ESSENTIALS
of Corporate
Governance

Essentials Series

The Essentials Series was created for busy business advisory and corporate professionals. The books in this series were designed so that these busy professionals can quickly acquire knowledge and skills in core business areas.

Each book provides need-to-have fundamentals for those professionals who must:

- Get up to speed quickly, because they have been promoted to a new position or have broadened their responsibility scope
- Manage a new functional area
- Brush up on new developments in their area of responsibility
- Add more value to their company or clients

Other books in this series include:

For more information on any of the above titles, please visit www.wiley.com.

ESSENTIALS
of Corporate Governance

Sanjay Anand

John Wiley & Sons, Inc.

Library of Congress Cataloging-in-Publication Data

Anand, Sanjay.
 Essentials of corporate governance / Sanjay Anand.
  p. cm.
 Includes index.
 ISBN 978-0-470-13981-3 (pbk.)
1. Corporate governance. I. Title.
 HD2741.A646 2007
 338.6–dc22   2007014934

Printed in the United States of America

10 9 8 7 6 5 4 3 2 1

To my wife

Contents

Contents

Foreword

I n 1886, a case was heard before the courts that forever changed the landscape of America. The ruling of *Santa Clara v. Southern Pacific Railroad* had the effect of creating a new being: the corporate entity. Although technically fictional and laden with legal jargon, the corporate being thus created has become so powerful that it is now ruling our everyday life.

I question whether, in creating a new entity to engage in societal activities and transactions, these decision makers considered sociological and psychological questions and weighed carefully their all-pervasive ramifications. Did they envision how this "being" would interact with the political and sociological forces of the twenty-first century? Did they consider, like a parent of a young child would, whether the new being would play fair and grow to become a responsible member of the community?

These are no longer fanciful questions. The morphing of knowledge society has changed the business environment as could never be imagined before. Business no longer is regarded as just an economic entity. It now has a ubiquitous role in society. Indeed it is an engine of socioeconomic transformation. Economic growth cannot be sustained without embracing the vast multitudes living in abject poverty and addressing the alarming depletion of our natural environment. With a fifth of the global population below the poverty line and global warming becoming a reality, issues like poverty alleviation and climate change have become the biggest business challenges of our time.

Corporate governance, which had been regarded as essentially an issue of statutory compliance with company law and listing requirements, has now become an instrument that governs the transparency, accountability, integrity, equity, and social responsibility in the decision-making process of the business.

Harsh sentences being meted out to Jeffrey Skillings, Bernie Ebbers, John Rigas, and Timothy Rigas are reminders that public expectations of the conduct of business have risen sharply. Nor are boards expected to be compliant simply through "box ticking." They have to be competitive and responsible. Corporate social responsibility and the triple-bottom-line approach have become today's mantras for business success.

The World Council for Corporate Governance was founded on the core belief of shared prosperity that goes beyond shareholder issues. It was the first one to start the process of engagement with stakeholders as a key to business success. It believes that the real value in a business is created by its customers, employees, suppliers, and the cooperation of civil society. Companies cannot make profit if customers won't buy their products. Linking business goal with larger societal purpose therefore helps align the human resource commitment and provides a significant competitive differentiator.

The World Council has been running various programs to help companies become competitive and improve the professional skills of the boards. Its star program is a five-day Masterclass for Directors. I have had the good fortune of knowing Sanjay as a meritorious participant of one of our Masterclasses when they began. I was deeply impressed by his insight on the issue of corporate governance. Since then I have shared many an international platform where both of us have been slated as keynotes. I am glad he has found time to author such a profound book, which is coming out at a time when the boards face the greatest threats and challenges of our times. I have no doubt that it will benefit readers from all walks of business life and provide a direction for sustainable business success.

Madhav Mehra

President

World Council for Corporate Governance

Preface

Corporations play a valuable role in our communities and in nations around the world. Good Corporate Governance is a union between the financial and personal success of a corporation. Strong profits and good business practices: These two concepts are integrally related, not disconnected from each other.

I could speak for hours about what good Corporate Governance is, and in truth, I often do speak for hours on the subject. Yet to define good Corporate Governance in just one sentence—the words elude me.

Since entering the world of business, I have watched good Corporate Governance develop into a dynamic and broadly encompassing concept. And I pride myself on the idea that I have made my own contribution to this evolution as well.

Good Corporate Governance is the idea of how best to run a corporate entity. It includes the management styles, the accounting principles, the model of ethical behavior, the openness of communication and, of course, the goings-on of the boardroom. Yet there is so much more held within this seemingly simple phrase—an energy of quality business ideals and doing a job to the best of our abilities—that no words can encompass.

While, I do not have just one sentence with which to describe good Corporate Governance. I have thousands of sentences at my disposal to help convey this business concept that is at the zenith of quality corporate life today.

Through my work with the Sarbanes-Oxley Institute, I have traveled all over the world assisting companies and professionals not only in complying with the Sarbanes-Oxley Act, but also in developing sustainable practices of good Corporate Governance.

What I have found eternally fascinating is the variety of policies and practices that are applied in different regions to achieve the same goal. This should tell us something: that good Corporate Governance is not a set of criteria but rather a process and an ideal. It is something that every corporation, in every market, can achieve.

This idea—that good Corporate Governance is a universal ideal—was my motivation in writing this book. And for that reason, I have striven to create a text that will be accessible and relevant to all levels, from corporate executives to private citizens, in nations around the world.

I can scan through my memory and play back the events in the good Corporate Governance timeline. From triumphs to scandals, the road has been exciting and eventful. We have come a long way toward stronger business practices, and I look forward to participating in the changes that are yet to come.

I hope this book empowers you to participate as well.

Learning Guide

Here is a summary of each chapter within this book. I have provided this to give you, the reader, some insight not only into what the chapters hold, but also why I chose these particular topics and what their specific relevance is.

I have designed this book to be a resource and reference guide, one that readers can return to time and again to answer their questions about Corporate Governance. The needs and interests of each individual will be different, and these summaries are meant to help you plan your own unique path through the information.

Readers will also find, within the appendixes, several resources that will keep good Corporate Governance concepts at their fingertips. One of my favorite items in this book is the glossary. More than a standard glossary, it provides a quick guide through the terms used most commonly in discussions of Corporate Governance and the world of business.

Chapter 1, Corporations. Before we can understand what Corporate Governance is, we must first understand the concept of the corporation. Chapter 1 provides insight into corporations in terms of their structure and function. This chapter also offers a brief overview of the ongoing debate regarding where a corporation's allegiances lie, and whether corporations are responsible solely to the shareholders or whether they have social responsibilities as well. This is the question at the heart of Corporate Governance because it speaks to the motivations of corporations and their boards in establishing Corporate Governance practices. By first examining why Corporate Governance is important, we will be in a better position to understand its implementation.

Chapter 2, History. Part of understanding where we are in terms of corporate regulation and behavior is understanding where we have been. Chapter 2 provides a brief outline of the history of U.S. corporate structure to arm you with the information you need as we move forward. One striking feature of this history is the noticeable tug-of-war between the government and the corporation. As we move through the decades, we can see a pendulum-like swing between freedom and regulation. In terms of a global perspective, it is important to realize that the U.S. model for corporations is only one of many. Each corporate structure has developed from the framework of the country in which it is situated. Economic pressures, social perceptions, and political events are all instrumental in creating each country's corporate model.

Chapter 3, Shareholders. As the legal owners of the corporation, shareholders have a vested interest in the company's financial performance. After all, it is their investment that will suffer if the corporation is not run in a profitable manner. Shareholders are in an interesting position in terms of Corporate Governance, and much discussion centers on how to best protect them from fraudulent behavior on behalf of the board of directors. Although this is certainly important, it is not the only consideration that Corporate Governance has regarding share owners. Shareholders own the company but are largely removed from the corporation's activities, which are left to the elected board of directors. In a legal sense, shareholders are neither financially responsible nor criminally responsible for the corporation's actions; however, Corporate Governance would see it otherwise. This chapter discusses shareholders, their role in the corporate structure, and their important involvement in Corporate Governance.

Chapter 4, Board of Directors. As the shareholders' representatives within the corporation, the board of directors functions as liaison between the interests of the shareholder and that of the executive. In Chapter 4 we discuss not only the structure of the board, but also how variations on that structure impact its ability to function effectively. The board of directors has many jobs, one of the most important of which is to monitor the executive. As the ones who appoint and evaluate the executive, the board of directors has a significant impact on the direction of the corporation and its ensuing success or failure.

The board also has a strong role to play in terms of Corporate Governance. Within their subcommittees, directors establish, monitor, and evaluate policies regarding financial reporting, remuneration, ethics, and member nomination. These responsibilities, and others of their kind, make the direction of the board of directors vital to a company's Corporate Governance efforts.

Chapter 5, CEO and Chairperson. Next to the board, a corporation's chief executive officer (CEO) is its most influential member. In fact, in some instances the CEO has even more power and authority than the board, but this stems from ineffective directors and a poorly established company hierarchy. In Chapter 5 we discuss the role of the CEO as well as some of the significant areas where problems arise—in particular, compensation and succession. Both how much a CEO makes and the process by which a CEO leaves the company and is replaced are complicated issues that every corporation struggles with.

There is a fine balance between the CEO who stays too long and the ones who leave too fast; the CEO whose resignation is voluntary and the one whose dismissal is demanded; and, of course, between overcompensating a CEO at the expense of the board and compensating sufficiently to draw viable talent. These issues are explored in this chapter to provide a background as we move forward to the core issues of Corporate Governance.

Chapter 6, Good Corporate Governance: An Introduction. Searching for the words to define Corporate Governance is a difficult task. This chapter seeks to elucidate this complex topic in order to make it clear that while Corporate Governance may have one definition today, it is an ever growing and evolving topic.

Instead of focusing on Corporate Governance as a phrase with a concrete definition, it is much more effective to think of it as a state of mind, a concept that is fluid and adaptable to the changing face of commerce.

Of course, this does not mean that there are no clear principles of Corporate Governance. It does mean, however, that as interested members of the business world, we have to be prepared to change our own impressions of the concept and adapt as it grows.

Chapter 7, Signs of Trouble. When a corporation falls to ruin, either by negligence or corruption, it is rarely the result of one isolated, short-term event. Instead, these situations arise as the consequence of months, or more often years, of neglect and ineffective governance on the part of the board of directors. In Chapter 7 we discuss several indicative events that point toward problems with the board of directors and its governance strategies. Although lengthy, this list is certainly not exhaustive. For as many boards and corporations that are in existence, there are as many opportunities for failed governance.

Reading this chapter will provide the bedrock for understanding why good Corporate Governance is important and the circumstances in which reforms are required.

Chapter 8, Changes Made through Corporate Governance. When a corporation elects to evaluate its Corporate Governance policies in an effort to improve itself, it is making a strong move forward. It is important to remember, however, that statistically speaking, good Corporate Governance does not necessarily correlate to high financial success for the company. Certainly there are instances in which companies are deemed highly successful in terms of their bottom line but have dismal records of Corporate Governance. Similarly, other companies are the shining examples of Corporate Governance but cannot manage to keep their heads above the financial waters. Although this fact may seem counterintuitive, it is not. Corporate Governance is only one of many components of a successful corporation. While good Corporate Governance will certainly not harm a company, it is not enough to create success. It is instead more useful to think of Corporate Governance as a means of facilitating prosperity rather than creating it.

Of course, companies that do not exhibit efforts toward improving their Corporate Governance, although they may be successful for a time, are at greater risk of falling to scandal, corruption, or negligence. In Chapter 8 we discuss the changes made through Corporate Governance that improve a corporation's ability to function effectively, thereby facilitating success.

Chapter 9, Regulations and Strategies for Corporate Governance. After garnering all of the necessary background information about corporations and their structure, it is time to delve into the issue at hand: Corporate Governance. Chapter 9 (as well as Chapter 10 for an international perspective) explains the principles of Corporate Governance, including the ways in which these principles impact all relevant parties. As the concept of Corporate Governance has grown in importance and spread in awareness, several leading sets of guidelines have been created.

Ideally, Corporate Governance will spread to create universal coherence in corporate practices. This does not mean that we expect every country, economy, or business to be run the same, but rather that each will adhere to a set of best principles and adapt them to their unique circumstances, thereby facilitating success while protecting rights.

The regulations discussed in Chapters 9 and 10 seek to guide countries and corporations in establishing their own good Corporate Governance policies. Throughout these guidelines, similar themes of integrity, accountability, stakeholder protection, and strong board independence can be seen.

Understanding these guidelines and the way that each one fits in creating a ubiquitous culture of good Corporate Governance is an important step in recognizing the importance of best practices and their implementation in individual corporations.

Chapter 10, International Corporate Governance. We begin our discussion of international Corporate Governance with an overview of its importance and the key concepts involved. As the global marketplace expands, it is becoming increasingly rare for companies and corporations to operate solely within the confines of one nation.

What is more common is for there to exist international partnerships, international subsidiaries, and foreign outsourcers. Further growing in popularity is the establishment of truly international corporations, whose existence is based between the borders of two or more countries.

When we speak of Corporate Governance, we are speaking of the corporation's efforts as a whole, not simply those efforts that are applied within just one country. Shareholders and society in general are becoming increasingly aware and involved in the international dealings of domestically based companies and are growing less tolerant of any perceived violations.

This chapter discusses the importance of international Corporate Governance practices, the challenges that arise in their implementation, and the organizations involved in facilitating their creation. The chapter also lays the framework for a more detailed discussion of international Corporate Governance.

Chapter 11, Corporate Governance in Emerging Markets: Asia and Latin America. Building on Chapter 10's discussion of international markets and their significance for Corporate Governance, Chapter 11 illustrates global Corporate Governance in terms of emerging markets and the efforts of corporations within them.

Although this chapter does discuss international regions, it does not delve too deeply into the concepts of international economies. Such a discussion would be neither feasible nor desirable within the context of this book.

Instead, this chapter delivers an overview of global economic relations and their consequences for good Corporate Governance policies. By discovering the general concepts through issues in Europe, Asia, and Latin America, the reader will be able to understand Corporate Governance in the international context.

Chapter 12, Not-for-Profit Organizations. Although discussions of good Corporate Governance and its issues primarily center on publicly traded companies and the protection of the shareholder, other organizations are recognizing the value and benefits of establishing good Corporate Governance practices.

Chapter 12 takes a look at not-for-profit corporations. Like publicly traded corporations, these organizations are chartered, but they are unable to sell shares or pay dividends. Also, like their for-profit counterparts, not-for-profit corporations also rely on voluntary investment by the public, although these actions are philanthropic rather than motivated by financial return. It is for this reason that not-for-profit corporations are taking a keen interest in Corporate Governance policies as a method of fostering public confidence.

PART ONE

Background

CHAPTER 1

Corporations

After reading this chapter, you will be able to

- Understand what a corporation is
- Understand how corporations are organized
- Understand the concept of capital structure
- Understand the concept of governance
- Understand the competing goals that corporations may have
- Understand why there is a call for corporations to be more ethical

Before moving directly into a discussion of good Corporate Governance, it is important to create a foundation based on the initial concepts of the corporation, its role in society, and its organization.

The corporation, like no other fictional entity, has created an unprecedented volume of debate and discussion. There are those who argue for its existence, its reform, and its abolishment. There are groups that study the corporation in terms of its sociological impact on individuals and those who study the corporation in terms of its impact on itself.

At the core of all meaningful discussions of the corporation is the concept of Corporate Governance.

This chapter discusses corporations in terms of defining what they are and how they are organized. This chapter also introduces the concept of corporate ownership, a theme that is carried throughout each part of this book.

In addition, readers will learn about theories suggesting the possible purposes of the corporate structure and the concept of corporate ethics. Finally, this chapter closes with an introduction into the concept of Corporate Governance as a nonnormative descriptive term used to express the method by which corporations are governed rather than the way in which they should be governed.

Corporate Structure

It is sometimes helpful to think about corporations as imaginary people. In many ways they do have the same rights and powers that the average citizen does; they are able to open bank accounts, file taxes, make purchases, and own property.

Unlike nonincorporated businesses that do these things under their company name, the corporation's assets are not directly owned by the company owner or partners. Specifically, when a nonincorporated business purchases property, the deed is held by the company owner. However, when a corporation does the same, the deed is held by the corporation itself.

Corporate Organization

Corporations are owned by stockholders who purchase shares and therefore own a percentage of the sum of the corporation's assets.

The stockholders elect a board of directors to represent their interests and govern the running of the corporation. The directors then appoint an executive to oversee the operations of the corporation. It is the role of the directors to govern the actions of the executive and ensure that the interests of the shareholders remain forefront in all decisions.

TIPS AND TECHNIQUES

Identifying Noncorporate Structures

In addition to the corporate structure, several other business forms exist. Two of the ones most commonly encountered are proprietorships and partnerships.

- *Proprietorships.* Businesses that are owned and run by one or more individuals.
- *Partnerships.* Businesses that are owned by one or more individuals and run by one or more of the same. This form is different from proprietorships in that not all owners need be involved in the operation of the business.

Corporate Ownership

Shareholders are the legal owners of the corporation. However, this concept of ownership carries roles and rights different from those commonly associated with the concept of private ownership.

In corporations, the roles of ownership and operation are separated. Shareholders may be the legal owners of the company, but they do not have control over its operations. As a result, they have no claim to the assets of the corporation, except in terms of dividend payment and asset division at dissolution. Beneficially speaking, this also means that shareholders are not personally liable for the debts of the corporation except to the extent that their stock value will be lost.

Benefits of Incorporating

Although companies all have unique reasons for seeking incorporation, one of the principal advantages is that assets of the corporation are not linked to the assets of the owners (shareholders).

Because the corporation is its own entity under the law, if it is sued or files for bankruptcy, the corporation is solely liable. This means that the corporation's assets can be redistributed through legal procedures, but the shareholders' personal assets are not assessed.

This is contrary to the situation of a nonincorporated business in which the business owner's personal assets can be seized in situations of civil or criminal litigation and bankruptcy.

 **IN THE REAL WORLD**

There are two types of corporations, C corporations and S corporations. One of the primary distinctions between these two classes of corporations is in terms of taxes.

C corporations are subject to two levels of taxation on income. First, the corporation itself is taxed on its revenue. When that revenue is

IN THE REAL WORLD (CONTINUED)

distributed to shareholders as dividends on their stock, a second level of taxation occurs.

The alternative is to form an S corporation, in which only one tax is applied. S corporations elect to have the corporate profits pass directly to the shareholders, without first being revenue of the corporation itself.

The major benefit of forming an S corporation is that a greater percentage of corporate revenue is passed to the shareholders as dividends because the amount is not first taxed.

Purpose of Corporations

There are many debates about the purpose of the corporation. These debates include questions about whose needs the corporation is designed to fulfill. Some believe that the corporation's sole purpose is to meet the needs of the shareholders, and that in doing so, everyone will be better off. Milton Friedman, author and economist, was one of the most notable proponents of this belief.

Others argue that the corporations should be accountable to not just the shareholders, but also their employees, the market members, and the community as a whole. Those who subscribe to this belief promote the ideology that corporations can create value for several factions that include, but are not limited to, the shareholders.

These two positions do not seem wholly irreconcilable. To meet the needs of the shareholder would mean that the corporation maximizes its share value. This would be done by building the most successful business possible, which could very well entail meeting the needs of other parties.

On the whole, there are several groups to which the corporation could be obligated, as shown in Exhibits 1.1 and 1.2. It is arguable that companies have duties to themselves, their shareholders, the economy, employees, and society as a whole.

Some of these duties include:

- *Needs of the corporation.* A duty to itself would entail the corporation's responsibility to sustain its own existence. This duty would include adherence to fiscal responsibility, the establishment of

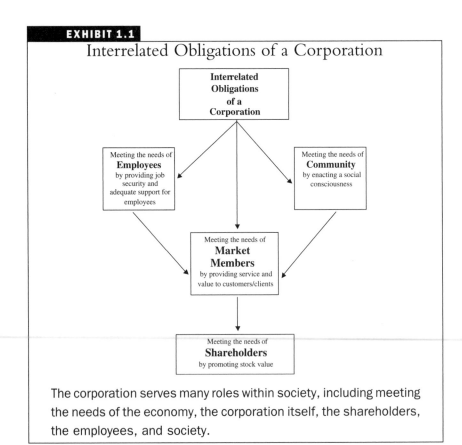

EXHIBIT 1.1

Interrelated Obligations of a Corporation

Interrelated
Obligations
of a
Corporation

Meeting the needs of
Employees
by providing job
security and
adequate support for
employees

Meeting the needs of
Community
by enacting a social
consciousness

Meeting the needs of
Market Members
by providing service and
value to customers/clients

Meeting the needs of
Shareholders
by promoting stock value

The corporation serves many roles within society, including meeting the needs of the economy, the corporation itself, the shareholders, the employees, and society.

EXHIBIT 1.2

Corporation's Interested Parties

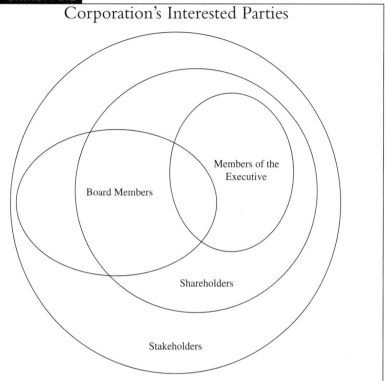

Within a corporation there are several overlapping groups of interested parties. The largest group, which encompass everyone with interest, are the stakeholders. There are also members of the board of directors who may or may not be shareholders and who may or may not be members of the executive. Similarly, an executive member may or may not serve on the board.

highly functioning boards and executives, and possibly avoidance of takeovers.

- *Needs of the shareholder.* That corporations have a duty to shareholders is not often disputed. Instead, debate arises regarding the extent to which this duty should be fulfilled. Corporations, their boards, and their executives must respect the corporate owners and work in favor of their interests.

- *Needs of the economy.* As embedded members of the economy, corporations may have a responsibility to the economy as a whole and others in its membership. Compliance with regulations that promote market health, such as the Sarbanes-Oxley Act and U.S. Securities and Exchange Commission guidelines, works toward fulfilling this potential duty.

- *Needs of the employees.* Outside of the American corporate structure, there are those corporations that consider the interests of the stakeholders rather than simply the shareholders. Within these corporate frameworks, the corporation has at a least a limited duty to provide for the interests of its employees.

- *Needs of society.* Discussions of corporations and their ethical responsibility all hinge on the question of whether they have a duty to society. Issues that would fall under this duty include considerations of the environment and activities in less regulated, emerging markets.

Irrespective of what a corporation believes that its duties are, or where its allegiances lie, it is clear that the existence of a corporation is inherently dependent on shareholders and their willingness to invest. Regardless of whomever else the corporation is obligated to, it must promote stock sales.

At the same time, corporations are not afforded the freedom to meet that duty by any means possible. It is reasonable to expect that their actions will be limited, certainly by the law and possibly by ethical considerations.

The Government, the Economy, and the Corporation

In this chapter we discuss the possibility that corporations have an obligation to meet the needs of the economy in addition to those of the shareholder. Whether or not corporations agree that they have such a duty, the government, in most instances, insists on it.

Government intervention and regulation of corporate activity is geared toward protecting the interests of the economy and the society while at the same time fostering successful business efforts.

The government's role is to balance the needs of several parties and demands, including:

- The employee, through the sustaining of a successful economy that provides jobs, but also through the establishment of regulations to ensure fair treatment, safe working environments, and minimum pay

- The consumer, through the fostering of a competitive marketplace that provides variety, but also against consumer fraud, hazardous products, and other consumer-related risks

- The environment, through the establishment of laws and policies that regulate hazardous materials, pollution, and other environmentally unsound practices

- The economy, through the establishment of policies that encourage market growth and investment while preventing accounting fraud and other activities that can be economically damaging

Frequently these needs are in direct competition with each other, and often the solution for one impedes the creation of the other.

Corporations and Ethics

That corporations have some level of ethical responsibility is almost universally agreed. Dissent and debate occur when the level of ethical responsibility is discussed, with some factions believing that corporate obligations do not extend past increasing share values and others arguing that as legal entities, fictional or not, corporations have ethical responsibilities.

Those who believe that corporations have ethical responsibilities argue that, because they are embedded within society and are capable of creating social and environmental impacts, they are ethically culpable for the outcomes.[1]

IN THE REAL WORLD

Nike, the Gap, and Public Dissent

There is a great deal of discussion in boardrooms and on the streets as to whether corporations are ethically responsible for their actions and, if so, the degree to which this obligation extends.

Irrespective of what theorists and corporations themselves decide, the public ultimately will determine whether corporations take stronger ethical considerations into account. In the end, the majority of most corporations are motivated by their bottom line. When consumers cease to consume in protest of unethical behavior, the corporate structure will adapt.

Over the past decade, we have seen stronger outcries on the part of consumers in regard to ethical treatment of the environment, workers in emerging markets, and other social issues. Two major poster children for unethical corporate behavior have been the Gap and Nike, both of which have received publicity for mistreatment of workers in developing countries.

Capital Structure

Corporations must have systems in place by which they finance themselves. In most instances these systems include some combination of equity sales, equity options, bonds, and loans. The exact formula used is different for each corporation, and every entity works to discover the optimal combination that provides the greatest stock value and lowest cost.

Governance

This book is dedicated to explaining and illustrating the importance of good Corporate Governance and the concepts that this entails. One of the first distinctions that must be made, however, is the distinction between the value-based definition of Corporate Governance and the practical-based one.

In terms of practicality, all corporations have policies of Corporate Governance; they all have management and boards of directors who govern the corporation's activities. From a practical standpoint, Corporate Governance does not have a value in terms of being right or wrong.

There is also the concept of Corporate Governance that reflects the judgment of what makes for good Corporate Governance and what makes for poor Corporate Governance. It is this definition that we will be using throughout the remainder of the book, but for now we will look at the principles of Corporate Governance as they apply to the basic governing of an organization rather than the proper, or good, governing of the same.

As the concept of the corporate organization has evolved, several models have emerged. Each of these models has been implemented in various markets, at various times, and with various degrees of success. All have their unique benefits and challenges.

- *Traditional model.* The traditional model is the most familiar governance model. This framework includes a board of directors that governs the activities of the executives (or management) who run the organization. The board will divide itself into smaller committees for completing specific tasks.

- *Carver model.* This model is similar to the traditional model; however, within the Carver model, the board of directors does not divide itself into smaller committees.

- *Collective model.* Conforming to the collective model requires that there be little distinction among the board, management, and staff in that all are involved in decisions and service delivery. This model is most frequently found in small organizations.

- *Operational model.* This model for Corporate Governance holds that the board of the company or organization will not only govern the activities but also run them. The operational model is most often found in charity or other not-for-profit associations in which the board runs an operation that is staffed by volunteers.

- *Management model.* This model is a step beyond that of the operational model in that the organization is run by the board, but includes a paid staff.

Conclusion

Corporations are often referred to as "a legal fiction," meaning that they are entities that do not actually exist but have legal significance anyway. This term reflects the fact that corporations are not human beings, but they do have some of the rights and powers that people have.

Many believe that as entities within our communities and the world at large, corporations should be subject to the same ethical and social standards that we apply to other citizens. Instead of being interested solely in the price of shares, corporations should be accountable to the environment, the community, their employees, and the state of the world.

Perhaps one of the simplest ways to think about corporations and their obligations is to consider them as having the obligation of meeting the needs of the shareholders within a framework that, at the very least, does not infringe on the interests of other parties.

Summary

- Corporations have similar abilities and legal responsibilities as human business owners.
- Corporate Governance can be discussed in terms of the model by which a corporation is run or in value-based terms of good versus bad Corporate Governance.
- The assets of a corporation are owned by shareholders and managed by the corporation's executive and board.
- There are two views as to whom the corporation has a responsibility: (1) the shareholders only, or (2) the shareholders as well as the community, employees, and the economy.

Note

1. Susan Ariel Aaronson, "Broadening Corporate Responsibility: Is Maximizing Shareholder Value Alone a Good Enough Long-Term Strategy?" *The International Economy* (2002).

CHAPTER 2

History

 After reading this chapter, you will be able to

- Understand how the corporate structure came to be
- Understand the various forms of corporate structure
- Understand significant events in U.S. corporate history

Vital to understanding where we are going is understanding where we have been. This is important not only to ensure that we do not make the same mistakes as our predecessors, but also to create a deeper understanding of things as they are.

Corporations and the corporate structure are integrally linked to the cultural environment in which they are built. It is because of each country's unique political, social, and economical landscape that corporate structure and practice vary so widely around the globe.

In terms of Corporate Governance and the U.S. corporate structure, the history is long and very eventful. The pages of this chapter disclose some of the most important events in the history of U.S. corporations. These events include the takeover eras, the 1929 stock market crash, corporate scandals at the turn of the millennium, and important corporate legislation.

The Early Years

One of the earliest of the modern corporations was the East India Trading Company, created at the turn of the sixteenth century. This corporation, like most others at the time, was created by the British Crown.[1]

In fact, in the early years, the United States was partially run by corporations, when some individual states were ruled by companies, such as the Massachusetts Bay Company.[2] After gaining its independence, the United States chartered corporations at the state level, but these companies were small and did not have the same autonomy as today's corporations.[3]

Types of Corporate Structure

The corporations of all countries do not all work in the same way. Having evolved in different economic and political climates, corporate structure varies around the globe. Although we discuss this concept in greater detail later, for now it is important to understand that the corporate structures we see in the United States are not the models seen elsewhere.

One of the most striking distinctions is that between the United States and Germany. In Germany, financial institutions are frequently large stakeholders in corporations, something that would not be seen in the U.S. model.

Historical Legal Landmarks

The history of Corporate America is marked by several significant historical landmarks. These events have helped to create the unique corporate structure found in the U.S. economy, just as events unique to other countries have shaped their corporate structures.

The rest of this chapter is dedicated to some of the largest and most significant of landmarks, but it is important to note that these are not the only ones. Every legal decision, corporate scandal, and economically significant event is a partial architect of a country's corporate structure.

Takeover Eras

The last notable takeover era was in the 1990s, but previous ones occurred in the 1900s, 1920s, 1960s, and 1980s.[4] Although appearing to occur at regular intervals, takeover eras are not scheduled events but rather triggered reactions.

Takeovers are common during times when the market has experienced a significant change. For example, the introduction of new corporate regulatory legislation or a significant technological innovation can trigger a takeover era. They are also seen after significant economic upheavals, such as a war or an energy crisis.[5]

Hostile Takeovers

In a hostile takeover, one company attempts to gain power over another without creating an agreement. In this strategy, the aggressor company purchases a high enough percentage of the company's shares to gain a controlling interest in it.

After acquiring enough shares, the aggressor company will start to displace former board members and slowly push all former company members out of their positions.

Victim corporations are not without recourse in situations of hostile takeover, although their options can be limited and bleak. Legally, there is a threshold of share ownership at which the aggressor company must state its intention of staging the takeover. At this point it is up to the corporation's current board and executive to take preventative measures.

The Poison Pill

One strategy to prevent a hostile takeover is to flood the market with shares in order to defeat the aggressor's attempt to acquire a majority. Specifically, the corporation offers only its shareholders the opportunity to purchase more shares for a negligible amount of money.

The Poison Pill strategy cannot be effective unless shareholders purchase the surplus stocks. Instead of supporting their current board and executive, shareholders may believe that selling their shares will provide the greatest return or that the corporation would be better in the hands of the aggressor company. See Exhibit 2.1 for more information.

The White Knight

In situations where a corporation cannot prevent a takeover from occurring, the board is still able to control the sale of the stocks if it can find what is known as a White Knight.

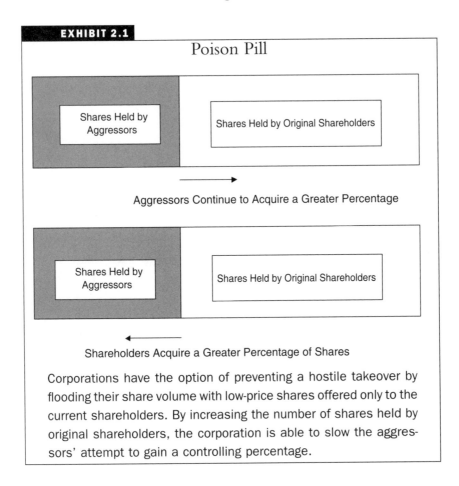

EXHIBIT 2.1

Poison Pill

Shares Held by Aggressors

Shares Held by Original Shareholders

Aggressors Continue to Acquire a Greater Percentage

Shares Held by Aggressors

Shares Held by Original Shareholders

Shareholders Acquire a Greater Percentage of Shares

Corporations have the option of preventing a hostile takeover by flooding their share volume with low-price shares offered only to the current shareholders. By increasing the number of shares held by original shareholders, the corporation is able to slow the aggressors' attempt to gain a controlling percentage.

A White Knight is an alternative purchaser who will enter the bidding war for the shares. The goal is that the White Knight will either drive the price of the shares up to provide greater value for those who sell, or that they (the White Knight) will acquire the corporation themselves.

Corporate Raiders

As in a hostile takeover, a corporate raid begins with the acquisition of a large volume of shares. However, unlike the takeover, the intent of a raid is not necessarily to take over the company. Instead the raiders may wish to simply gain a controlling interest.

Santa Clara v. Southern Pacific Railroad

The 1886 *Santa Clara v. Southern Pacific Railroad* court case established the legal designation of corporations as similar to persons. It is due to this ruling that corporations are considered legal, fictional beings that have the same rights and abilities under the law as do humans.

This ruling has several ramifications that are apparent in corporate structure. One consequence is the fact that corporations are able to purchase properties and hold deeds in their names rather than in the names of the owners. Another consequence is the government's ability to tax the revenues of corporations at the company level, rather than waiting until they are passed to individuals.

Stock Market Crash of 1929

The stock market crash of 1929 was the result of corporate corruption and marked the end of a bull market. The Great Depression ensued, a time of high unemployment and low economic activity.

An added consequence of the market crash was investors' loss of trust in the public markets. The New Deal, created by the federal government, was an effort to restore that market faith and foster the rebuilding of the U.S. economy.

Securities Act of 1933 and Securities Exchange Act of 1934

As a direct result of the crash of 1929, the U.S. government passed two pieces of legislation, the Securities Act of 1933 and the Securities

Exchange Act of 1934. Each act was designed to help the government create tighter regulations on corporate activities and protect the public from corrupt behaviors.

The Securities Act of 1933 established regulations by which the integrity of Corporate America would be rebuilt. In a related move, the Securities Exchange Act of 1934 established the Securities and Exchange Commission (SEC) to oversee the act's implementation.

Securities and Exchange Commission

The SEC was established through the enactment of the Securities Exchange Act of 1934, following the crash of the U.S. market. The principal goal of the SEC is to regulate corporate activities through policy development, compliance guidance, and information gathering.

To facilitate its mandate of protecting shareholders from corporate corruption and false accounting practices, the SEC requires that all publicly traded companies regularly disclose specified information through the submission of various forms.

Corporate Scandals of the 1990s and 2000s

At the turn of the millennium, the public witnessed several major corporations' fall to corruption. The court cases, bankruptcy filings, and civil suits that followed were the results of various instances of insider trading, inaccurate financial reporting practices, and other corrupt activities.

As with the stock market crash earlier in the twentieth century, this onslaught of fraudulent activity shook the public's faith in the integrity of publicly traded corporations. The Sarbanes-Oxley (SOX) Act is a direct consequence of these cases.

Sarbanes-Oxley Act

Following several notable examples of corrupt accounting practices in the 1990s, the U.S. government drafted and passed SOX in 2002. The purpose of this act is to protect investors and establish accounting guidelines to create greater transparency in the financial reporting practices of corporations.

In addition to explicating standards for corporate executives, accountants, and auditors, SOX also created the Public Company Accounting Oversight Board (PCAOB), which works in partnership with the SEC to govern corporate activity.

Conclusion

The economic history of the United States has been marked by battles between the government and corporations to find a happy balance between freedom and regulation. Although corporations originally were developed to serve the interests of the British Crown, and later the U.S. government, they are now independent and, in a legal sense, autonomous entities.

Summary

- Corporations were first charted to serve the bidding of the British Crown.

- The type of corporation seen in the United States is only one example of corporate structure. Other forms exist, having evolved in different political, social, and economic circumstances.

- Corporations gained elaborate freedom and rights in the ruling of *Santa Clara v. Southern Pacific Railroad.*

- The Securities Act of 1933 and SOX were both designed to create greater government regulation of corporate activities.

Notes

1. Lee Drutman, *The History of the Corporation.* Citizen Works Corporate Power Discussion Groups, http://www.citizenworks.org/corp/dg/s2r1.pdf.
2. Ibid.
3. Ibid.
4. European Corporate Governance Institute (ECGI), "Research Digest," *Research Newsletter: Corporate Takeovers* 1 (Spring 2006).
5. Ibid.

PART TWO

The Players

CHAPTER 3

Shareholders

After reading this chapter, you will be able to

- Understand what shareholders are and their role in a corporation
- Understand the basic rights of shareholders
- Understand the duties that the board of directors has to shareholders
- Understand the types of ownership
- Understand the importance of shareholder meetings

Shareholders purchase stock within a corporation and are the legal owners of that corporation's assets. This is a unique feature that corporations have in comparison to many other companies: The owner does not run the company.

There are several consequences of the corporate structure and its segregation of ownership from operation. This chapter explores what it means to be a shareholder as well as the unique factors that contribute to the positions, rights, responsibilities, and risks.

The discussion relates to issues that include information disclosure, board elections, shareholder meetings, and the fiduciary duties owed to stock owners.

Ownership and Responsibility

As the legal owners of the corporation, shareholders are entitled to secure their investment by participating in the company's activities, although their involvement is limited. Shareholders are not involved in the operations of the corporation, except through their election of the board of directors and voting on proposals. Additionally, those who own stock, although technically they have purchased a portion of the company's assets, have no access to those assets. Instead, the real value of the stocks is limited to dividend payment, share resell, and potential asset value division at the dissolution of the corporation.

Given the minimal control that shareholders have over a corporation, it is important that they be granted sufficient opportunity to secure their investments. The rights of shareholders include the right to receive information, the right to elect board members, and the right to submit and vote on policy proposals.

Receiving Information

Shareholders expect that they will receive accurate and representative information regarding the corporation's policies and particularly its financial situation.

These communications are offered to shareholders by way of the annual shareholder meeting as well as through reports that are released on annual and quarterly schedules.

Shareholders must also be assured that they are receiving all important information related to issues that arise between the releases of reports. The U.S. Securities and Exchange Commission (SEC) facilitates this through Form 8-K.

TIPS AND TECHNIQUES

When to File Form 8-K

The U.S. Securities and Exchange Commission requires the filing of Form 8-K in circumstances when material changes occur within the corporation and its operations. For these purposes, a *material change* is anything that does or may create a significant impact on the company's financial situation. Although this requirement is not new to the corporate world, the enactment of the Sarbanes-Oxley (SOX) Act did increase the situations in which submission is required through SOX Section 409.

A complete list of specified situations in which corporations must inform shareholders and the SEC follows.

- Changes in company control
- Acquisition or disposition of significant assets
- Bankruptcy or receivership
- Certifying accountant changes
- Director resignation
- Code of ethics modifications
- Entry into a material agreement that is not in the ordinary course of business

TIPS AND TECHNIQUES (CONTINUED)

- Termination of a material course agreement that is not ordinary
- Creation of a material obligation under an off-balance-sheet arrangement
- Triggering events that accelerate or decrease a direct financial obligation or off-balance-sheet arrangement
- Costs associated with exit or disposal activities
- Material impairments
- Failure to satisfy a continued listing rule or standard
- Changes or restatements of previously issued financial statements, related audit reports, or completed interim reviews

Board Elections

Shareholders vote to elect board members who they believe will take good care of their investment in the corporation. In most situations the shareholders vote on potential candidates who were nominated and screened by the sitting board members.

It is also possible for shareholders to nominate potential directors themselves, but these nominees will have to be screened by the board before being included on the ballot.

Some problems that can arise and create an insufficient system in terms of electing appropriate representation include inadequate information about prospective directors and an inability to nominate candidates.

TIPS AND TECHNIQUES

Appointing a New Board Member

The board of directors is charged with the responsibility of governing the corporation on behalf of the investors. With the title "board member" comes great responsibility as well as an increasing amount of liability. As such, the election of a new member is not generally taken lightly.

In an ideal circumstance, when the term of a director ends, this process should occur:

- Determine if the incumbent director would like to apply for reelection.
- Determine if the incumbent director is suitable for reelection in terms of history, current circumstances, and the circumstances of the board and corporation.
- Begin the search for new director nominees, requesting nominations from shareholders, executive members, and other members of the board.
- Screen potential nominees and create a short list.
- Establish a recruitment strategy for potential nominees and create a finalized list of eligible and willing candidates.
- Communicate the identities and profiles of nominees to shareholders before the annual shareholder meeting.
- Submit the list of director nominees to the shareholders at the annual shareholder meeting.

Proposal Submission and Voting

Throughout the fiscal year, shareholders are able to submit proposals to help direct the corporation in the direction that they deem fit. These proposals, as well as those put forward by the board, are voted on by the body of shareholders.

Several protocols are consistently required for shareholder proposals. Without adherence to these protocols, the proposals will not be considered by the board. However, even when the protocols are met, the board may use its discretion in presenting those matters to the shareholding body for voting.

The rules governing shareholder proposal submission include:

- The shareholder must own at least 1% of the company's stock, have owned it for at least one year, and must commit to continual ownership through the voting date.

- The shareholder may not submit more than one proposal per voting period.

- The proposal may not be more than 500 words in length and must not relate to any prohibited proposal content.

IN THE REAL WORLD

Changing Level of Shareholder Involvement

Whether the change has been sparked by corporate scandal, education regarding their rights, or a new breed of active shareholders moving in, the message is clear: Shareholders are no longer willing to be passive members of the corporation.

Because shareholders are the lawful owners of the corporation, there is a great deal of discussion regarding shareholder rights and the obligations that boards and executives have in meeting them. But what about the shareholders' responsibilities in sustaining those rights?

In The Real World (continued)

In most situations, shareholders have the right to put forward and vote on proposals. They have the right to nominate and elect board members. And they have the right to form advocacy groups to support their own cause. The corporation itself should not hinder or prohibit these efforts because they are fundamental to the investors' ability to protect their investment.

Unfortunately, shareholders themselves sometimes can inhibit the effective exercise of their own rights. In the past, shareholders often have neglected their voting privileges, have been hesitant to submit proposals, and have adopted an overall passive attitude regarding the running of the company.

Times are changing, and in just three years, the number of shareholder-initiated proposals increased 87%.[1]

Within some corporations, shareholders are offered the option of purchasing stocks that do not carry voting rights. The incentive for purchasing these stocks is generally financial.

In the Real World

Shareholder or Stakeholder?

There is a clear distinction between *shareholder* and *stakeholder*. A shareholder is someone who has purchased the stock of a publicly traded company. However, a stakeholder can be considered to be anyone who has a vested interest in a company.

This means that while shareholders are stakeholders, not all stakeholders own shares. For example, volunteer members of nonprofit associations can be considered stakeholders, although there are no shares involved.

IN THE REAL WORLD (CONTINUED)

With this distinction come differences in responsibilities and rights. Because the term *stakeholder* is nonspecific and applies to several types of interested parties, it is clear that not all stakeholders warrant the consideration given to shareholders. For example, a shareholder may expect to vote in board elections, but not all stakeholders of a company are entitled to this privilege.

Duty of Loyalty and Duty of Care

To protect shareholder interests, the board is assigned two fiduciary duties: the duty of loyalty and the duty of care. The extent to which the board meets these duties can be taken as a measure of its effectiveness.

- *Duty of loyalty.* In keeping with the duty of loyalty, the board and its members are required to act on behalf of shareholder and company interests, rather than their own.

- *Duty of care.* This duty requires that company directors make reasonable efforts to care for the company's interests.

Board members who do not meet either of these duties are subject to reprisal through shareholder petition for dismissal, class action suits, or legal injunction. It does occur, and has occurred frequently in the past, however, that reasonable avenues have not been available to shareholders to deal with violations of duty.

Shareholder Meetings

Shareholder meetings are held to provide shareholders with a forum in which to gain information and cast votes. Although designed to ensure that investors are able to actively protect their investments, shareholder meetings can be largely unproductive when not run effectively.

Conclusion

As the legal owners, shareholders are a fundamental part of the corporate structure. Their position as owners is unique, however, in that they do not hold legal or financial responsibility over the corporation's actions or events. Shareholders also have limited avenues available to them for monitoring corporate activity and being involved in the company's decisions.

Summary

- Stockholders are the legal owners of a corporation.
- Stockholders vote in the election of the board of directors who run the corporation.
- The elected board of directors has a responsibility to its stockholders that includes adherence to the duties of care and loyalty.

Note

1. Diane K. Schooley, Celia Renner, and Mary Allen, "Corporate Governance Reform: Electing Directors through Shareholder Proposals," *CPA Journal Online,* www.cpajournal.com (October 2005).

CHAPTER 4

Board of Directors

After reading this chapter, you will be able to

- Understand what the board of directors is and its primary functions

- Understand the duties of a corporation's board of directors

- Understand the importance of independent outside directors

- Understand the process of electing the board of directors and important considerations in doing so

- Understand the issues surrounding director compensation and reprisals

- Understand the role of subcommittees within the board

Central to the functions of a corporation is the board of directors. These are the elected company members who have been delegated, by the shareholders, to oversee the corporation and the executive on their behalf.

At their best, boards serve as a governing body within the corporation and keep the executive on track in terms of meeting legal and financial obligations. Unfortunately, this is not always the case, and some boards neglect their duties, opting instead to function as "yes-sayers," agreeing to all executive decisions without consideration of the outcomes.

Several factors can impact the efficacy of a corporation's board of directors. Its size, the fairness of the election system, and the inclusion of independent members all have an impact on how well a board is able to govern. Other factors include the profiles of the members; the diversity of expertise that is represented by the board; and the commitment that the directors have to monitoring the corporation's activities.

Overall, when an effective board has been elected, it will be successful at monitoring the corporation and helping facilitate the company's ability to meet both long- and short-term goals. The board does so by reviewing the actions and decisions of the executive, evaluating remuneration plans, and detecting deficiencies in effective governance.

This chapter delves deeply into the concept of the board of directors. As the body charged with governing corporate activity, the board is central to all discussions of Corporate Governance.

 TIPS AND TECHNIQUES

Jobs of the Board

Members of the board of directors are elected by and represent the shareholders. The directors function as the voice of the share-

Tips and Techniques (continued)

holders—the owners—representing their interests in the corporation's events, decisions, and activities. Some of the specific jobs assigned to the board include:

- Developing long-term goals for the company
- Monitoring and replacing the chief executive officer (CEO)
- Monitoring and replacing other key members of executive management
- Reviewing and evaluating compensation plans for executives and directors
- Monitoring governance strategies
- Detecting incompetence within the board itself
- Selecting and screening board nominees
- Communicating with shareholders
- Monitoring for conflicts of interest

Structure

No one-board profile will fit the needs of each and every corporation. Instead, the perfect composition of the board will be a direct reflection of the corporation's unique structure and needs.

In most cases, the specific framework for the board's structure will be established by the corporation's bylaws. In some circumstances, however, the structure of the board will have to change in order to accommodate new developments within the corporation, such as growth or merger.

In general, a board's profile is comprised of its size, ratio of independent members, ratio of executive directors, segregation or unification of the chairperson and CEO positions, and subdivision into committees.

- *Size.* Although there are no specific requirements on the size that a board has to be, in some circumstances a board can be too small or too large. For example, a board that is too small will not have the expertise or humanpower available to run the company productively.

  However, a board that is too large may be inefficient at making and implementing decisions. A board that is too large can also waste resources and diminish individual productivity. Large boards can be managed, however, by subdividing members into subcommittees.

- *Chairperson.* The chairperson is responsible for heading the activities of the board, including governance of corporate operations. In some corporations, the same person serves as chairperson and CEO.

- *CEO.* The role of the CEO is similar to that of the chairperson in that the CEO is the leader of the executive, as the chairperson is the leader of the board. There is a great deal of debate regarding the dual function of the CEO as chairperson of the board. The consensus is that the interests of the corporation are best served when these titles are separately held.

- *Executive members.* The principle of board independence can also be threatened when a high percentage of the directors are also members of the executive. This can lead to conflicts of interest in important board decisions, such as executive evaluations and compensation.

Executive directors are members of the board who function full time within the company and serve as board members. With the election of executive directors come both benefits and downfalls. On the positive side, these directors offer strong insight into the operations of the corporation and have a great deal of background knowledge and experience. Executive directors also have relationships and lines of communication established with other members of management and corporate staff.

Executive directors create concern for a few reasons. First, some believe that when a CEO sits on the board, the value of the board will be negated by merging its interests too closely with those of the executive. Second, it may not be possible for lower executive members to evaluate their superior (the CEO) objectively while functioning as board members.

A large component of this risk is the fact that executive directors are used to reporting to the CEO in their role as members of the executive. In situations where they have to act in a manner that contradicts the CEO, these directors may be torn between their duties as board members and loyalty to the CEO. They may also fear that contradicting the CEO could materially damage their career prospects.

IN THE REAL WORLD

Board Structure in Germany

Just as the corporate structures established in different countries vary, so do the structures of the board of directors. In the Anglo-American corporate structure, the board of directors serves as the

IN THE REAL WORLD (CONTINUED)

shareholders' representation within the corporation. However, in other corporate structures, boards serve different functions.

In Germany, for example, boards are generally structured in two tiers: an executive board plus a board that oversees the executive board. German boards also differ from those within the Anglo-American structure in that they contain labor representatives. This requirement is indicative of Germany's stakeholder, rather than strictly shareholder, focus.[a]

[a] European Corporate Governance Institute, *Research Newsletter: Effective Boards,* vol. 3 (2006).

IN THE REAL WORLD

Chairperson and CEO, or Chairperson-Slash-CEO?

Within a corporation, there are two prescribed roles for strong leadership. The first is the chairperson of the board, who is charged with governing all of the board's activities, including its regulator functions over the executive. The second leadership position is that of the CEO, who leads corporate operations and is in charge of the activities of the executive.

Within the corporate hierarchy, the chairperson has greater standing than the CEO does, in that when there is a disagreement between the board and the executive, the will of the board is expected to stand. It is arguable, however, that the role of the CEO is more important on the grounds that if the CEO performs his or her job with complete success and perfect adherence to all rules and regulations, then the role of the chairperson of the board will become superfluous.

Responsibility of Selecting the CEO

One role of the board of directors is to select a CEO to fill the position as it becomes available. The strategy for choosing a new CEO consists of careful evaluation of the candidates, establishment of an effective recruiting strategy, strong communication and support regarding the change, and careful evaluation of the new CEO.

Evaluating the Candidates

In theory, candidates for the CEO position can come from anywhere. In reality, however, these candidates are likely to come either from within the company's own management team or from that of a close competitor. It is very rare for a CEO to come from an unrelated industry or a nonmanagement position.

In evaluating the candidates, the directors will consider several factors including experience, past performance, personal attributes, leadership skills, reputation, and compatibility with the company. Furthermore, the directors will also look for a candidate who will stay with the company for a significant amount of time rather than one who is likely to leave quickly.

Effective Recruiting

The successful appointment of a CEO is dependent on the corporation's ability to secure the prospect's interest. Just as the board considers several factors when selecting the CEO, the candidate must consider various issues when deciding whether to accept the position.

A prospective CEO will evaluate the company in terms of:

- *Its history and reputation.* The candidate will want to ensure that his or her professional reputation will be helped, not harmed, by accepting the position.

- *The compensation package.* The compensation package includes not only salary, but also bonuses, stock options, and benefits. One argument in favor of high CEO compensation rates is that the remuneration is a key factor in recruiting quality CEOs.

- *The relationship of the executive and the board.* A board that is too overbearing and infringes on the executive's ability to run the corporation will not impress a CEO.

IN THE REAL WORLD

Creating an Heir

It is not unusual for a CEO to select and mentor a successor, someone to fill his or her shoes when the CEO steps down.

In the best situations, the candidate recommended by the former CEO will assume the position with relative ease and minimal

Responsibility of Selecting the Executive

One of the principal responsibilities of the board of directors is the selection and appointment of executive members, including the CEO. Intricately related to this function is the board's role of governing the executive and taking action when the executives' activities do not coincide with the best interests of the corporation and its shareholders.

In general, the process for selecting and appointing executive members is similar to that of nominating new directors. The board requests that directors and other trusted parties submit recommendations. From those recommendations, the board creates "short lists" of candidates based on credentials, experience, and availability. Recently there has been a significant trend toward favoring candidates who come from within the corporation's management structure.

Those potential appointees who make the "short list" are assessed through a process of discovery, recruitment, and interviews. Considerations of their future prospects, potential conflicts of interest, the reactions of major stakeholders, and the opinion of current board and executive members will all have an impact on the final selection.

Legal Obligations

In most states, a corporation's board of directors has a legal obligation to meet a duty of care and a duty of loyalty. Although these duties are primarily in regard to the shareholders, they do have ramifications for all aspects of corporate activity.

- *Duty of care.* Directors have an obligation to make decisions for the corporation that are reasonably representative of the company's and shareholders' best interests. This means that the directors must support their decisions with sufficient evidence, as well as be responsible for obtaining that information.

- *Duty of loyalty.* This duty prohibits directors from putting their own interests ahead of those of the corporation or the shareholders.

- *Duty not to entrench.* This duty prohibits the board from establishing policies and practices that prevent directors from being removed from the board, even in circumstances where their presence is hindering company success.

- *Duty of supervision.* Working along the same lines as the duty of care, the duty of supervision elaborates on those principles and requires that the board facilitate its own discovery of corporate operations and executive activity.

IN THE REAL WORLD

Business Judgment Rule

Although boards are required to adhere to the duties of care and loyalty, this does not mean that they are necessarily liable for

Independent Outside Directors

An effective board must contain a balanced mix of members both from within the company and from outside. This ensures that the board remains independent and objective, thereby maximizing its ability to make decisions that are in the best interests of the corporation.

Of course, the efficacy of having independent directors on a board depends on their active participation and willingness to monitor the board's activities. Independent directors who are unmotivated or too busy to fully commit to their duties will not further the board's independence.

In some circumstances, the corporate structure, other board members, or company executive can hinder the functional abilities of independent directors. For example, in order to maintain active involvement, independent directors must have access to all necessary corporate information.

Depending on the circumstances, independent directors may need to meet with members of the executive, to review financial records, or to be informed about other corporate activity. When other company members or the structure of the corporation itself inhibits access to such information, the efficacy of the independent board members is greatly hindered and the abilities of the board are hindered as well.

Busy Board Members

Board members, particularly independent ones, sometimes sit on the boards of several organizations. The greatest benefit of such "busy" board members is the varied experiences and skills that they are able to offer.

There are obvious downsides, however, that result from board members who have spread themselves too thin. Independent directors serve a valuable role in maintaining the efficacy of the board and its ability to monitor the executive. When their attention is divided among several organizations, their function on any one board can become limited. A board that contains too many directors who are multiboard members could suffer from reduced independent representations.

Foreign Board Members

As the global economy expands, it is becoming more important for boards to include independent directors from countries other than that in which the corporation is based. This is particularly valuable as a sign of board independence in those companies that have a high percentage of foreign shareholders.

Elections

Generally speaking, it is impossible for shareholders to run a corporation directly. In most cases, the body of people who own a corporation's stock is very large. There is also the fact that purchasing stock does not mean that the shareholder has any business expertise or the ability to run a company.

For these reasons, shareholders elect qualified directors to sit on the corporation's board and make decisions on their behalf. The election of board members is one of the principal rights and duties that a shareholder has, and with it comes a great deal of responsibility.

Unfortunately, there is also a great deal of opportunity for corruption within the board election process. Sometimes shareholders are not provided with adequate opportunity to vote, enough information on the nominees, or the ability to nominate members themselves.

As the stewards of the company, its actions, and its financial performance, the board of directors is paramount in the corporation's success. This is why shareholder votes in board elections have become a targeted issue for corporate reform in recent years and a primary focus in Corporate Governance.

Nominations

Each year, at the annual shareholder meeting, shareholders are afforded the opportunity to vote on incoming directors to the board. The candidates are those who have been selected by the board's nominations committee from a pool of recommended nominees, as shown in Exhibit 4.1. Those nominated will include successful recommendations from the executive, the board, the shareholders, and outside stakeholders.

To guarantee a fair and informed process, the nomination committee must ensure that the shareholders receive sufficient information

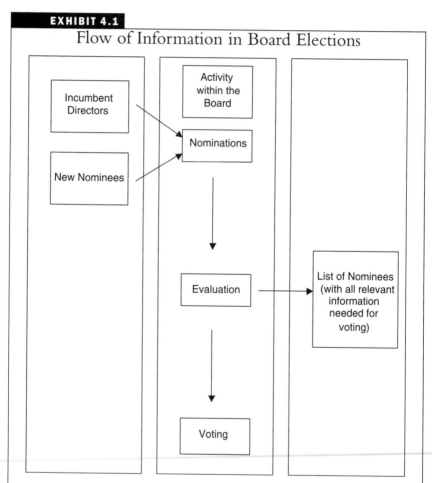

EXHIBIT 4.1

Flow of Information in Board Elections

The process for electing members of the board involves a flow of information both into and out of the incumbent board. The board must take recommendations from outside sources, and also must provide information to the shareholders.

about each candidate and that the information is sent well before the meeting date.

Voting

The election of directors generally occurs during annual shareholder meetings. In order to provide fair representation, votes are usually weighed on the "one share, one vote" principle.

Compensation

The members of the board of directors are compensated by the company. There are several possible methods for compensation, and the specific packages are usually a combination of salary, stock options, and bonuses.

- *Director salary.* The salary level of directors is determined by the compensation committee and varies widely between corporations. In situations where these salaries are apparently lofty, justification arguments appeal to competition for quality members and the importance of a strong board.

- *Stock options.* It is important that members of the board be compensated, in part, with packages that include company shares. The simple logic behind this requirement is that doing so encourages the directors to behave in the best interests of the shareholder, by making those interests their own.

- *Restricted stock.* Restricted stock has limited trade provisions associated with it. These restrictions serve to prevent insider trading and other stock-related scandals.

- *Liability insurance.* Members of the board of directors do risk legal and financial liability for corporate activities. In some circumstances, board members are provided with liability insurance as part of their compensation package. Although such a practice does increase the value of the packages, it may also lead to reduced motivation for ensuring ethical and legal behavior.

IN THE REAL WORLD

Compensating with Liability Insurance

Members of the board of directors risk legal and financial liability for corporate activities. In some circumstances, board members are provided with liability insurance as part of their compensation package. Although such a practice does increase the value of the packages, it may also lead to reduced motivation for ensuring ethical and legal behavior.

Reprisal

Just as shareholders are able to elect directors to the board, they are also expected to be able to remove them. Should the stockholders have a substantiated belief that a director is not behaving appropriately or is violating any fiduciary duties, they are able to petition for the director's dismissal, enact a class action suit, or seek a legal injunction.

In most countries, board members are also able to call for the dismissal of any members who are not meeting their obligations. This process can be difficult and arduous, however. Further exacerbating the problem is the issue of director entrenchment, where board members cannot be removed because of corporate policy or convention.

For example, in the past, board members often were reelected automatically at the end of their term. This has been one method by which poor directors have been able to remain on boards despite being ineffective. There are two solutions to remedy this problem.

The first and more radical solution is the establishment of set limited terms. These are predetermined periods after which board members are ineligible for reelection. The second, more moderate, approach is to eliminate conventions that lead to automatic reelection or renomination.

IN THE REAL WORLD

Sarbanes–Oxley Act

The enactment of the Sarbanes-Oxley (SOX) Act created guidelines for auditors, corporations, executives, and boards of directors. These guidelines are meant to ensure accurate reporting practices to protect the interests of investors and prevent financial misrepresentation.

As a result of SOX, company members, including directors, now carry greater liability when investors are misled, by either fraud or neglect. The act also mandates the establishment of an audit committee that contains a high percentage of independent members, one of whom must be an accounting professional.

Additional Committees

To help facilitate its ability to monitor the corporation's activities, the board of directors often is subdivided into smaller committees. These committees allow for more focused activity and discussion, especially in situations where the board has a large membership.

An additional benefit of establishing committees is that it allows directors with specific expertise to contribute within their prescribed areas. Common board committees include the audit committee, compensation committee, nominating committee, and governance committee.

- *Audit committee.* A company's audit committee is a necessary establishment under the Sarbanes-Oxley Act and the regulations of the U.S. Securities and Exchange Commission (SEC). This committee works to ensure that the financial reports released by the company to the SEC, the shareholders, and the general public are accurate and representative.

  In keeping with these responsibilities, the audit committee generally monitors the establishment of the corporation's financial controls and oversees the work of accountants, both internal and out of house.

- *Compensation committee.* Because the compensation committee is required to review the compensation practices of the corporation, it is vital that its members are not unduly influenced by the executive, other board members, the CEO, or any other controlling interests.

  Circumstances in which such influence arises could represent a violation of the directors' duty of care. To combat such a risk and ensure that stockholder interests are being represented, corporations are legally required to disclose the compensation values and how the amounts were chosen.

- *Nominating committee.* This subdivision of the board of directors serves to establish board membership criteria and nominates directors for election or reelection.

- *Corporate governance committee.* This committee is responsible for establishing a monitoring policy relating to Corporate Governance. In this capacity, the nominating and governance committees work together to ensure that the board meets its duties to shareholders and works toward the best interests of the corporations.

TIPS AND TECHNIQUES

Duties of the Compensation Committee

The compensation committee is a subdivision of the board of directors that is responsible for establishing and monitoring the corporation's remuneration packages and policies. Its specific responsibilities include:

- Evaluation of executives' performance
- Approval of compensation levels
- Approval of bonuses and other incentives
- Review and approve severance agreements
- Evaluate director compensation

In the case of all committees, careful consideration and planning must occur on the part of the board to prevent conflicts of interest. It is possible that directors who serve on multiple committees could be making decisions or functioning in capacities that are at odds with their role on another committee.

TIPS AND TECHNIQUES

Establishing an Ethics Committee

The ethics committee serves as a watchdog over the actions of both the executive and the board itself. An effective ethics committee will function to establish, monitor, and prevent. The expected actions and responsibilities of the ethics committee include:

- The committee should establish ethical standards and procedures. Doing so may require rewriting current standards, composing new codes of ethics, and reevaluating current education strategies.

- The committee should continually monitor the corporation's ethical compliance. This can involve reviewing corporate activities to ensure that they comply with ethics standards as well as establishing a system for dealing with infractions.

- The committee should have procedures and guidelines in place to be able to prevent infractions from occurring when risks are identified. This can be achieved through effective monitoring.

Conclusion

The board of directors serves a valuable and important role within the corporation as the liaison between the interests of the shareholders and those of the executive. When an efficient and effective board is established, it works to ensure that the corporation is compliant with the policies of the SEC as well as other important legal requirements.

In terms of Corporate Governance, the board and its committees have the capacity to monitor the corporation's efforts and establish policies to spearhead greater compliance. Because of these important functions, it is vital that the board's structure be one that facilitates effective policy discussion and voting. That is why board size and composition must be carefully considered and monitored.

Summary

- The board of directors is the shareholders' representative within the corporation.

- Executives are appointed and evaluated by their board.

- The board's composition, in terms of size, percentage of independent directors, and director profile, will greatly determine its efficacy.

- Frequently boards are subdivided into committees to facilitate efficiency and capitalize on areas of director expertise.

CHAPTER 5

CEO and Chairperson

 After reading this chapter, you will be able to

- Understand the significance of the role of the chief executive officer (CEO)
- Understand the distinction between the CEO and the board chairperson
- Understand the issues surrounding CEO compensation
- Understand the importance of careful planning in regard to CEO succession

The CEO is a board-appointed member of a corporation's management team. The primary role of a CEO is to run the company in a successful manner, thereby securing the interests of shareholders and the value of their stocks.

CEOs are necessary members of the company, because they, unlike shareholders or even board members, have the specific experience and education to run the daily events of the corporation.

There are times when the board and the CEO disagree about what decisions are in the best interest of the corporation. When disagreements such as these occur, the decision of the board is meant to veto that of the CEO. This organizational structure stems from the internal hierarchy of the corporation; the board defers to the shareholders, and the executive defers to the board.

This chapter discusses the concept of the CEO as it relates to corporate structure, relationships with the board, and distinctions from the role of the chairperson.

Understanding the expectations of the CEO, the issues surrounding compensation, and CEO succession practices is integral to creating a complete picture of corporate structure. Reading these pages will provide the final piece in terms of the key players involved in good Corporate Governance practices.

Role of the Chairperson

The chairperson is responsible for the organization and activities of the board of directors. This position is elected by the shareholders at the annual shareholder meeting.

In terms of desirable characteristics, an ideal chairperson will exhibit exemplary ethical and moral standards. He or she will also possess strong leadership skills and have the ability to manage the board effectively.

Finally, it is also desirable that the chairperson have the ability to facilitate strong communication and mutually respectful relationships between the board and the executive and the board and the shareholders.

IN THE REAL WORLD

Duties of the Chairperson

The chairperson of the board is responsible for heading all board activities as well as leading board meetings. Some of the specific duties include:

- Running the board and establishing the agenda
- Facilitating the ability of board members to receive accurate and timely information on which to base their decisions
- Protecting the rights of the shareholders to receive accurate and timely communications regarding material events
- Facilitate shareholders' ability to communicate with the board to ensure that directors have a clear idea of shareholders' interests
- Ensure that the board as a whole, its members, and its committees are evaluated annually

Expectations of the CEO

A corporation's CEO is appointed by the board to spearhead the management of the corporation. In selecting a new CEO or evaluating a current one, the board will look for several key characteristics that are generally considered desirable:

- *Strong performance record.* When selecting a CEO, the board will look at the candidate's performance record in his or her current and past positions. In doing so the committee will want to see a strong trend of successes. This trend would relate to promotions, personal achievements, and relevant experience.

In a similar manner, a board that is evaluating the performance of the current CEO will be best served by looking at long-standing trends rather than just recent accomplishments or challenges.

- *High level of experience.* Although a potential candidate need not have experience in the capacity of serving as a CEO, it is desirable that the candidate have other relevant experience that will facilitate the shortening of their learning curve in their new role.

It is generally accepted that an ideal CEO candidate should have experience in management and leadership, experience in the relevant industry, and experience within the corporate frame-work.

In terms of evaluating the experience of an incumbent CEO, the board will want to look at the efforts made by that officer toward improving his or her expertise and abilities. These efforts can include workshops, courses, seeking new partnerships, and other modes of self-improvement.

- *Strong interpersonal skills.* A corporation's chief executive officer must be able to relate to several corporate members on varying levels. The CEO must communicate with shareholders, company employees, members of management, and, of course, members of the board of directors.

The CEO of a corporation is also frequently looked on as a spokesperson for the company. It is therefore beneficial if he or she has a strong media presence and is comfortable dealing with the press.

Although interpersonal skills can be difficult to ascertain through introductory meetings, the candidate's track record and profile will speak to his or her abilities.

Boards can evaluate the interpersonal skills of their current CEO fairly easily, given that they likely have a great deal of personal experience to draw from. However, efforts should be made to determine the relationships that are present with others as well, in order to formulate the most objective evaluations possible.

Executive Compensation

As misdeeds of executives become increasingly publicized, shareholder interest in executive compensation grows. No longer do shareholders have blind faith in the decisions of the board; instead they require documentation and evidence.

Of particular concern are situations in which compensation decisions are compromised by conflicts of interest. As a result, many corporations are disclosing more information than in the past to reassure shareholders.

Further aiding in the spirit of disclosure are the rules of the U.S. Securities and Exchange Commission (SEC). Shareholders are now privy to the process by which the board's compensation committee develops the packages. This means that shareholders can evaluate their board's decision using all of the same information used by the board. (See Exhibit 5.1.)

- *Base salary.* A CEO's salary is really only the starting point for how much he or she actually makes. Often the salary is relatively small compared to the additional benefits and bonuses.

EXHIBIT 5.1

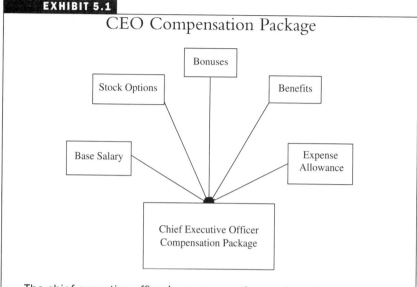

CEO Compensation Package

The chief executive officer's compensation package is designed to lure the best and brightest candidates that the corporation can afford. In order to maximize the package's effectiveness, a combination of compensation products are offered.

- *Benefits.* Unlike others in the employment market, a CEO's benefits package has few limits. The benefit packages can include health and dental, retirement, insurance benefits, transportation, vacation, and many other, sometimes surprising, items.

- *Expense allowances.* In the name of conducting business, CEOs are often afforded extravagant expense accounts for entertaining clients, travel expenses, and various memberships.

- *Bonuses.* Generally, bonuses are task-based rewards that are presented to the CEO upon achieving a particular goal or set of goals.

- *Stock options and grants.* Most compensation packages include some incentive for the CEO to purchase the corporation's shares.

Agency Theory

In the early to mid-1900s, Adolf Berle and Gardiner Means wrote influential works, independently and as a team. Perhaps best known for their work regarding Corporate Governance, these men wrote extensively on the concept of agency theory.

Agency theory explains the fact that when principals charge agents with the task of running their businesses, the principals will generate less revenue than if they did so themselves.

Of course, this relation between the principals and the charged agents is contingent on factors such as whether the principals have equal or greater ability to run the business, but, in general, it reflects the theory that motivation of personal gain will increase productivity.

Based on agency theory, recommendations toward aligning the interests of the principals with those of the agents have been developed. These recommendations include mandatory stock ownership by directors and executive members as well as the establishment of compensation policies that are linked to corporate performance.

Board–Management Relationship

Several scenarios can play out between the executive and the board. Walking into boardrooms across the United States would provide a glimpse at all of these, as they are all present in some capacity in today's corporate culture.

The models for board–management relationships include the board as governor, the board as "yes-sayer," and the board as meddler.

We will take a look at each of these scenarios starting with the least desirable yes-sayer and meddler, and moving to the ideal scenario of the governor.

- *Yes-sayers.* The board of directors has a clear charge to appoint an executive body and govern its activities to ensure that the interests of the shareholders are being met.

  A board that completes only half of its task is a liability to the corporation, insofar as it appoints an executive but makes no efforts toward effective governance.

  Situations such as these enable the executive to have free rein, thereby negating the entire purpose of establishing a governing board within the corporation.

  Overly complacent boards are becoming less common, however, as stronger precedents are being set toward director liability.

- *Meddling boards.* One of the principal reasons that the board appoints an executive is that the board itself is generally not able to oversee the operations of the company directly, because of both a lack of skill and an ineffective structure.

  Instead, it is the role of the board to govern the operations by overseeing the actions of the executive, questioning motivation and reasoning when it seems suspicious, and establishing policies to guide the corporation's overall direction.

  There are circumstances, however, in which the members of the board will either hijack the role of the executive or create so many operational boundaries that effective operation of the company is simply not possible.

Just as a board that is inactive in its role of governance is a liability for a corporation, so is a board that is overactive in its efforts.

Of course, few corporate board–executive relationships are as clearly defined as these scenarios. In reality, most boards exhibit some components of each with one tendency that may be stronger than the others.

CEO Succession Planning, Selection, and Performance

We discussed the concept of entrenchment earlier in the book. Like boards, CEOs can also become entrenched well past the time during which they are successful in running the company. When CEOs have outlived their usefulness, it is said that their term has run too long.

However, there are also situations in which a CEO's term can be too short. It is clear that the CEO has a very important role in the company. Understandably, a CEO departure creates significant ramifications for the corporation, the board, and the shareholders. That is why it is in the best interests of the corporation, the board, and the shareholders that the CEO position is not subject to quick turnover.

CEOs depart from companies for many reasons. These can be amicable departures that are planned, such as retirement. A departure can also be the result of the CEO's own choice.

IN THE REAL WORLD

CEO Severance Packages

In January 2007, The Home Depot dismissed its CEO, Robert Nardelli, with over $200 million in severance.

Shareholders were understandably concerned, not only with the large severance at a time when their shares' values were falling, but also with the apparent corporate loyalty to Nardelli, both during his term and dismissal.

During his last years as CEO, Home Depot shareholders saw their shares drop 20%.[a]

[a] Hannah Clark, "Blame the Board," *Forbes Magazine Online* (2007), www.forbes.com.

TIPS AND TECHNIQUES

Term Limits

There are plenty of examples from the past in which CEOs of corporations have overstayed their time of usefulness. This overstaying can result in ineffective running of the company and the possibility of lost revenue.

In situations where CEOs, or any members of management and the board, remain in their position too long, they are said to be entrenched. Many boards have worked to prevent the threat of entrenchment by establishing bylaws that include term limits.

A term limit is a predefined time at which the CEO's position will be ended, irrespective of his or her performance. Although term limits are beneficial in that they prevent lengthy entrenchment, they can

Conclusion

Although it is the board that is primarily responsible for the company's well-being, the CEO is still a significant player. Given the importance of the role, it is clear why so much of the discussion regarding Corporate Governance centers on the CEO.

Summary

- A corporation's CEO is appointed by the board to run the company.

- The decisions of the CEO defer to the board, and in situations of disagreement, the board's ruling should stand.

- CEO compensation packages are determined by the board based on recommendations made by the compensation committee.

- Shareholders take a great interest in executive compensation levels, especially those of the CEO. They are particularly sensitive to conflicts of interest and incongruities between bonuses and profits.

- Because the CEO is a vital figure within the corporation, CEO succession must be carefully planned in order to maintain company stability during times of change.

PART THREE

Good Governance

CHAPTER 6

Good Corporate Governance: An Introduction

After reading this chapter, you will be able to

- Understand the concept of Corporate Governance
- Understand why Corporate Governance is important
- Understand the contributing factors that lead to corporate crime
- Understand the models of Corporate Governance
- Understand the principles of Corporate Governance

A corporation is established within a clear hierarchical framework. The corporation is owned by the shareholders and run by the executive. Between these two parties lies the board: the group elected by the shareholders to represent their interests and oversee the running of the company.

The board is responsible for appointing the executive. It also is responsible for monitoring the executive's progress, behaviors, and outcomes. This means that an ongoing problem within the executive represents a deeper issue: a problem with the board.

The board of directors can fail in its duty to oversee the corporation's affairs in several ways. The board can be ineffective at detecting and rectifying problems within the executive. It can also fail in its duty when its members forget their allegiance to the shareholders and instead serve the interests of the executive or themselves.

Whether purposeful or accidental, a board that neglects its duty to watch over the company and represent the interests of shareholders should not be able to continue in the same manner. Allowing it to do so could result in activities and events akin to those seen in the corporate accounting scandals of the 1990s.

Corporate Governance is the principle by which the board is expected to effectively oversee and direct the activities of the corporation. Implementing effective Corporate Governance principles will ensure that the interests of shareholders are represented and that the corporation will meet all of its legal and ethical requirements.

This chapter introduces the concept of good Corporate Governance and illustrates its importance in the general corporate culture. Through a discussion of the good Corporate Governance practices and who they benefit, readers will be able to situate corporate members in terms of their relationship to Corporate Governance.

Readers will also find that these pages contain useful theoretical content that explains not only the foundations of good Corporate Governance, but also possible culprits for ineffective efforts and the resultant culture of corruption.

Definition of Corporate Governance

A truly complete and representative definition of Corporate Governance can be elusive; many have struggled to find the words and phrasing that will capture everything that Corporate Governance is. Corporate Governance is a broad and complex concept that incorporates almost every aspect of corporate life.

Further compounding the complexity of Corporate Governance is the fact that this term has grown and evolved to encompass questions of ethical duties to employees, communities, and the world at large. Where once we spoke of Corporate Governance in terms of fiscal responsibility and accurate accounting practices, now the conversation includes environmental activity, employment practices, and political involvement.

We can break Corporate Governance down in terms of who it benefits, whose interests it reflects, who is responsible for it execution, and who it has the greatest impact on.

- *Shareholders.* Essentially Corporate Governance protects the interests of the shareholders because it ensures that the corporation is run with their best interests in mind. The original concept, that Corporate Governance is meant to ensure accurate accounting principles and truthful reporting practices, still holds, no matter how the definition of Corporate Governance expands.

Irrespective of what other issues we include in Corporate Governance discussions, the truth remains that corporations are owned by shareholders and it is their interests that must be met, because without their investment the corporation will cease to prosper.

However, shareholders are not simply beneficiaries of good Corporate Governance practices; they are involved in the process as well. Since Corporate Governance is ultimately measured in how well the corporation meets shareholder needs, it is up to those who own company stock to remain vocal advocates for themselves.

TIPS AND TECHNIQUES

Prohibiting Conflicts of Interest

In terms of Corporate Governance, a "conflict of interest" is any situation whereby a person would have an ulterior motive for his or her action. For example, if an independent board member sits on the boards of two corporations that are entering dealings, a potential conflict of interest exists. It would be very difficult for this board member to view the situation objectively and meet the best interests of both corporations simultaneously.

Internal conflicts of interest can also occur. Within the board of directors, subcommittees often are established to govern specific areas of the board's activities. Board members who sit on multiple committees must ensure that their work does not overlap in a way that could taint their ability to make objective decisions.

TIPS AND TECHNIQUES (CONTINUED)

In a culture of suspicion, as in today's post-Enron world, it is not enough for company board members not to have actual conflicts of interest; they must also eliminate any perceptions of such. This means that red flags may still be raised at the appearance of a conflict of interest, even if it is possible that an individual can remain objective in his or her situation.

For this reason, it is advisable that boards and executives carefully observe the kinds of personal and business relationships in which they are involved and the perceptions that these can create.

The Organization of Economic Co-operation and Development (OECD) recommends that companies offer complete information regarding possible conflicts of interest that may arise and the manner in which they are being dealt with.[a]

---

[a] Organization for Economic Co-operation and Development, *Corporate Governance: Frequently Asked Questions about the OECD Principles of Corporate Governance,* www.oecd.org.

- *Board members.* The board of directors and its members are ultimately responsible for the establishment and execution of good Corporate Governance strategies.

  As shareholder representatives within the company, their ability effectively to govern the executive will determine how well the principles of Corporate Governance are met. This means that the board must have sufficient independence or the ability to counter the decisions of the executive.

- *Executives.* As the company members in charge of running the corporation, the executives are the group with whose activities Corporate Governance is primarily concerned. A corporation's Corporate Governance practices are going to dictate the behaviors of the executive and the manner in which they are monitored. It is not necessarily the case that a company with strong Corporate Governance practices will have a board that is highly involved with the executive. On the contrary, part of good Corporate Governance is appointing a capable executive who will run the company effectively without the board babysitting him or her.

Basics of Corporate Governance

One of the most fundamental components of good Corporate Governance is the establishment of an effective company hierarchy. This means that the shareholders, board members, and executive, as well as their respective relationships, must all be organized in a manner consistent with Corporate Governance principles.

Communication between the board/executive and the shareholders must be able to inform those who own stock of relevant company events and decisions. It is also vital that shareholders have a reasonable method of communicating their grievances and opinions on applicable matters.

Similarly, the board and the executive must have not only open lines of communication for information and discovery, but also adequate separation to ensure that their roles are distinct. This means that the board must include independent members outside of the executive so that the board's governing function does not become compromised.

Finally, the relationship between the executive and board must not be so intertwined that the executive is unable to run the corporation effectively. Although the board's makeup should reflect a variety of skills and experience, the executives are generally more adept at managing the business, and the board–executive relationship should not hinder that ability unnecessarily.

It is because of these complicated relationships that corporate structure and communication are so important in effective Corporate Governance. If even one party is prevented from performing his or her role, the mechanism as a whole becomes compromised. For example, Corporate Governance can break down when shareholders do not have access or are unwilling to access information regarding their investment. Likewise, when the board is organized in a manner that does not facilitate monitoring of the executive, members are unable to ensure that the needs of the shareholders are being met and are essentially useless in terms of the company's Corporate Governance efforts.

TIPS AND TECHNIQUES

Who Benefits from Good Corporate Governance?

A corporate structure in which good Corporate Governance flourishes is one that has the potential to benefit all who are involved. See Exhibit A.

- The shareholders benefit because their needs are fairly met.
- Board members benefit because their role is clearly defined and the board is organized in a manner that facilitates effective functioning.

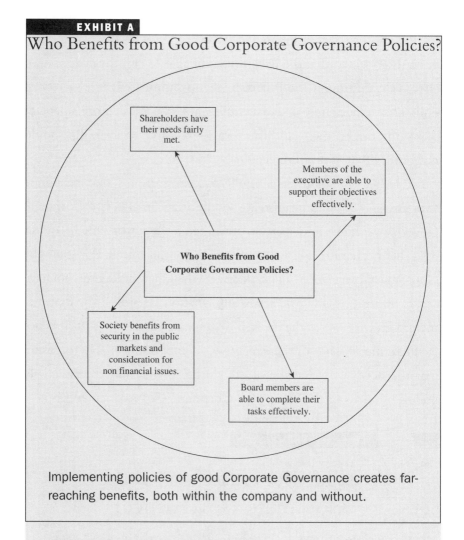

EXHIBIT A

Who Benefits from Good Corporate Governance Policies?

Shareholders have their needs fairly met.

Members of the executive are able to support their objectives effectively.

Who Benefits from Good Corporate Governance Policies?

Society benefits from security in the public markets and consideration for non financial issues.

Board members are able to complete their tasks effectively.

Implementing policies of good Corporate Governance creates far-reaching benefits, both within the company and without.

TIPS AND TECHNIQUES (CONTINUED)

- Members of the executive, including the Chief Executive Officer, benefit because they have systems in place to support their objectives and the support of the board behind them.

- Employees benefit because their roles are clearly defined and their jobs are not as likely to be threatened by poor management.

Theories of Corporate Governance

In 1932, Adolf Berle and Gardiner Means cowrote *The Modern Corporation and Private Property.*[1] In this book they argued that the separation of ownership from management within corporations created managerial economy in which the interests of the managers could supersede those of the shareholders.

The discussions and arguments attributed to Berle and Means hinge on the concept of dispersed share ownership in which many shareholders have only small stock holdings. This is not generally the case in many Asian and European countries, and is only marginally common in terms of the U.S. market.[2]

Agency Theory

A concept strongly related to Corporate Governance, "agency theory" refers to the best practice for organizing the relationship between the principal and the agent. This theory was a large component of Berle and Means's discussion of Corporate Governance. In their context, shareholders are the principals, while managers are the agents.

One of the key principles of agency theory is the concept that agency loss occurs in the corporate structure. "Agency loss" refers to the amount of money that principals (i.e., shareholders) "lose" by not running the corporation themselves.

The theory further elaborates on methods of reducing agency loss by aligning the interests of shareholders with those of the corporation's management. Such strategies include requisite stock ownership for management and gradient compensation that works on a scale of the corporation's success.

Theorized Causes of Corporate Crime

There are many theories as to why so many corporations have fallen to negligence and scandal. Popular theories in the media are those related to greed and personal corruption. Of course, when one objectively evaluates these crimes, one easily sees that corporate scandal extends far beyond those players directly involved.

Historically, the most popular theories regarding corporate scandal have come from the fathers of the concept of good Corporate Governance, Berle and Means. In *The Modern Corporation and Private Property*, they argued that scandals arise because although we may charge corporate managers with the responsibility of acting in shareholders' best interests, they are still capable of acting on their own.

In order for one or more individuals to behave unethically, their actions must be condoned, ignored, or otherwise facilitated by negligence on the part of other company members. Frequently, it is ineffective governance that enables scandals to occur.

The belief that the corporate organization itself spawns the corruption is not new. In fact, this theory was made famous in 1949 by E. H. Sutherland in the study *White Collar Crime.*[3] In this study Sutherland emphasizes that in looking for the cause of corporate corruption, the search must begin with the organization itself.[4]

Another increasingly popular theory is that the U.S. corporate culture as a whole breeds corruption by overstating the importance of continual increases in profits and decreases in overhead. Further contributing to this culture is the increasingly iconic image of the chief executive officer (CEO).

As current and past CEOs, such as Richard Branson, Steve Jobs, and Bill Gates, accumulate wealth, they also accrue fame. In many situations, the CEO becomes synonymous with the company. This can create difficulty for the board in its efforts at governance.

IN THE REAL WORLD

Corporate Scandal

Although perhaps the best-known scandals of Corporate America are those of Enron, WorldCom, and Tyco International, they are far from the only ones. In fact, they are not even the only ones of the infamous years at the turn of the twenty-first century.

The number of corporations that have had to restate their profits has risen sharply for the past two decades. In the early 1980s, only a handful of corporations restated their accounts. Ten years later, that number jumped to almost 100. In another 10 years, 2002, 250 U.S. public companies required statement adjustments. Between the years 1997 and 2001, the Xerox Corporation embellished its profits by $1.4 billion.[a]

---

[a] Jian Chen, *Corporate Governance in China* (New York: RoutledgeCourzon, 2004).

Models of Corporate Governance

As the concept of Corporate Governance has evolved and the importance of good Corporate Governance principles has become increasingly accepted, several models have emerged. Each of these models has been implemented in various markets and with various degrees of success. All have their unique benefits and challenges. Here is a brief recap of these models alluded to earlier:

- *Traditional model.* The traditional model is the most familiar governance model. This framework includes a board of directors that governs the activities of the executives who run the organization. The board divides itself into smaller committees for completing specific tasks.

- *Carver model.* This model is similar to the traditional model. However, within the Carver model, the board of directors does not divide itself into smaller committees.

- *Collective model.* Conforming to the collective model requires that there be little distinction between the board, management, and staff in that all are involved in decisions and service delivery. This model is most frequently found in small organizations.

- *Operational model.* This model for Corporate Governance holds that the board of the company or organization will not only govern the activities but also run them. Although not acceptable as a model for publicly traded corporations, the operational model is found in not-for-profit associations in which the board runs an operation that is staffed by volunteers.

- *Management model.* This model is a step beyond that of the operational model in that the organization is run by the board, but it includes a paid staff.

Principles of Corporate Governance

Corporate Governance is a concept that is best served by focusing on the end rather than the means. Put another way, because the rules and guidelines of Corporate Governance are always changing and evolving, it is important that we do not get so caught up in the procedures that we forget the goal.

The goal of good Corporate Governance is to establish an effectively organized management structure and activity system that will facilitate the corporation's ability to meet the needs of shareholders and any other pressing needs that may arise.

Corporations that focus on meeting the principles of Corporate Governance through the guidelines, rather than simply meeting the guidelines, will find themselves better able to move with the changing times. Those principles are:

- *Independence.* Corporations can achieve good Corporate Governance practices only when their boards are sufficiently independent. This means that there must not only be separation of the roles of CEO and chairperson, but also that the board of directors must contain a high percentage of independent members who are active in their role. A corporation with a strong Corporate Governance structure must have an independent board of directors. Without board independence, there cannot be effective governing of the executive, and the directors will be unable to meet their fiduciary duties to shareholders.

87

- *Accountability.* One of the benefits of a corporation is that the owners have limited or no liability beyond that of their investment. In past years, this lack of liability has expanded into a general sense of lawlessness for individuals in the corporate structure.

  All members of the corporate structure must be willing to be held accountable for any failings created either by their actions or by negligence.

  New regulations and governing bodies are focusing on reestablishing a sense of accountability within corporations. Doing this means ensuring that members know not only their responsibilities, but also the extent to which they will be held liable should they neglect those responsibilities.

  In order to facilitate this principle, it is advisable that corporations establish clear codes of ethics and job descriptions so that all corporate members have clear ideas of their expectations. For example, the board's fiduciary duties to the shareholders are a form of accountability. Similarly, the CEO is held accountable for accounting practices by the Sarbanes-Oxley Act.

- *Responsibility.* In addition to being held accountable, corporate members should also be held responsible for their duties and obligations. This means that it is their responsibility to ensure that they have all of the necessary information required to make the right decisions or complete their tasks successfully.

- *Reputation.* To keep Corporate Governance in perspective, we must remember that it is not only about fostering good business practices, but also about creating a strong relationship between the corporation and the public.

Corporations that work to build their reputation as companies that strive for good Corporate Governance practices benefit from increased loyalty and trust on the part of shareholders. By focusing on building a strong relationship rather than simply complying with regulations, corporations will stay ahead of changing codes and laws.

Conclusion

Although Corporate Governance is a complex issue that is still in need of a clear definition, the principles of the concept and those who are responsible for its implementation are clear. Corporate Governance is the idea behind effective management relationships among shareholders, the board, and the executive of a corporation.

One important concept that is not addressed nearly enough is the fact that good Corporate Governance is not necessarily synonymous with a profitable corporation. Although it is intuitively correct that truly effective Corporate Governance will help rather than hurt profits, the reverse is not necessarily accurate: Companies with poor Corporate Governance can be profitable.

This fact is perhaps one of the motivators behind the external establishment of Corporate Governance guidelines; it is done to provide nonfinancial incentives for good Corporate Governance practices. Several of these guidelines have been created throughout the global economy. Although these guidelines vary in their implementation and execution, for the most part, they subscribe to the same basic principles of independence, responsibility, accountability, fairness, and reputation.

Summary

- The board of directors is ultimately responsible for the establishment and execution of a company's corporate governance practices.

- Narrowly speaking, "Corporate Governance" refers to the relationship between the corporation and the shareholders, and the ability of the company board/executive to meet the shareholders' needs.

- Many people have made efforts to expand the concept of Corporate Governance to include the responsibility of the corporation to meet the needs of employees, other stakeholders, and society in general.

Notes

1. Adolph Berle and Gardner Means, *The Modern Corporation and Private Property,* reprint ed. (Piscataway, NJ: Transaction, 1997).

2. Jian Chen, *Corporate Governance in China* (New York: Routledge Courzon, 2004).

3. E. H. Sutherland, *White Collar Crime* (New York: Holt, Rinehart and Winston, 1949).

4. Carl Keane, "The Impact of Financial Performance on Frequency of Corporate Crime: A Latent Variable Test of Strain Theory," *Canadian Journal of Criminology* 35, no. 3 (1993): 293–308.

CHAPTER 7

Signs of Trouble

After reading this chapter, you will be able to

- Understand the indicators of corporate troubles that relate to the board of directors
- Understand the danger signs that can be seen in the attitudes and activities of the corporation's executive
- Understand the indicators of danger visible in the profiles and activities of the shareholders
- Understand the problem indicators shown by a corporation's financial records

When a corporation falls to corruption or negligence, it is not usually an overnight event. Instead, the demise of the company generally is preceded by several years of poor governance on the part of the board and a failure to represent the needs of shareholders effectively.

This chapter is dedicated to explaining some identifiable signs that commonly precede major governance challenges for an organization. Each of these indicators is linked to negligence, incompetence, or poor judgment on the part of the board of directors.

These indicators are arranged in terms of those that relate to the board of directors themselves, the executive members, the shareholders, and the corporation's overall well-being. The ability to identify these signs of potential trouble can be useful for those looking to invest in or otherwise involve themselves with a company. It can also help company members who are seeking to evaluate their corporation and its need for Corporate Governance policy reform.

Indicators Relating to the Board

In evaluating the strength of a company, one of the first places to look is the board of directors. This recommendation is based on the fact that without a strong board, the company cannot hope to have a strong practice of good governance. Danger signs of the board include:

- *High turnover of board members.* A corporation that has difficulty maintaining board membership is demonstrating either an already existing problem or the danger of a future one. A board of directors that loses members frequently could be demonstrating symptoms of infighting, militant factions, poor compensation, or one of many other problems. Not only are these issues problems for the corporation in and of themselves, but they are also likely to create further problems by destabilizing the board.

The role of a director requires skill, knowledge, and familiarity with the corporation. A company that often loses board members prematurely may suffer from an inexperienced board, which could result in poor efficiency, diminished productivity, and a greater risk of uncontrolled executive powers.

A high turnover rate is particularly indicative of a problem when it occurs in key board positions, such as the chairperson or committee leaders.

- *Board entrenchment.* The opposite of high turnover is entrenchment of directors, which can be just as dangerous. Low change rate of board members from one term to the next despite poor corporate performance indicates that the members have secured their positions irrespective of the company's needs.

  A corporation with an entrenched board is at greater risk of ignoring the needs of shareholders, instead serving the agendas of the board members themselves or members of the executive.

  Several corporations have included anti-entrenchment provisions as components of their charters and bylaws. A danger of these provisions is that they often rely on limited terms. Although limited terms do prevent entrenchment they can also create inexperienced boards. By setting fast rules for how long board members may serve, the corporation risks dismissing effective directors too early.

- *Recruiting difficulties.* The health of the board of directors is reliant on the corporation's ability to recruit talented and experienced board members. A corporation that experiences difficulties in this arena may be unable to provide competitive compensation due to financial difficulties. Problems with recruiting can also indicate a poor reputation for the board in terms of director treatment or institutional barriers that prevent board members from doing their job effectively.

- *Poor attendance at board meetings.* An ongoing pattern of poor meeting attendance by board members is an indication of an ineffective board. This is especially true in situations where there is also a failure to deal with the absenteeism.

    The board of directors has an extremely important role within the corporation, and that role cannot be fulfilled without active and meaningful involvement of the directors. An absent board is a strong indication that there is poor governance of the executive.

- *Back-room deals.* A high level of back-room dealings and lack of open communication among members of the board of directors is an indication of unhealthy director relationships. These back-room deals can also precede significant decisions and policy implications that reflect the interests of individual directors rather than the interests of shareholders.

- *Open disdain or distrust between board members and CEO.* Although the board of directors is ultimately responsible for the corporation, it delegates the operations to the executive members, whom members of the board appoint.

    Since the board members appoint the CEO and other executive members, it is a danger sign when the relationship deteriorates to one of distrust or disdain. This can indicate that the board was not sufficiently independent to appoint the executive members of their choosing or that the CEO has become entrenched.

- *A fractured board.* Often, especially with large boards, directors gravitate to smaller groups. This is desirable when these groups are in the form of functional committees and benign when they are simply pods of like-minded directors who do not seek to dominate or bully other directors.

  There are situations, however, where the board will contain two or more clear factions of directors working against each other. This is never a desirable situation within a board as it can impede productivity and is often indicative that the interests of shareholders are not being represented effectively.

- *Conflicts of interest.* Whether actual or apparent, conflicts of interest are dangerous. Failure to address conflicts of interest that arise, and poorly managed policies for their identification and elimination, can indicate an ineffective board. Furthermore, sustained conflicts of interest represent a high risk that the interests of others than those of shareholders are influencing board decisions.

- *Insufficient independence.* The independence of the board of directors is an integral component of good Corporate Governance. In order for the board to monitor and evaluate the activities of the executive objectively, it must contain members who are not also involved in other areas of the corporation.

  It is important to note, however, that inclusion of independent board members is not sufficient for the creation of an independent board. True independence also requires that independent members' involvement in board committees and decisions be facilitated by the corporate structure.

Situations in which communication with independent board members is inhibited or their inclusion in board decision-making activities is inhibited can be indicators of a nonobjective board.

- *Failure to comply with policies.* When the board of directors continually fails to comply with its own policies, including ethical policies and those relating to decision-making processes, it is an indication that the board has become entrenched and is serving its own interests.

  A similar situation is one in which the corporation's board fails to comply with the company's charter and bylaws, especially when such failures are ignored.

- *Poor communication with investors.* Whether the result of intentional secrecy or institutional barriers, a lack of communication between the board of directors and shareholders is an indication of poor Corporate Governance.

  When shareholders are not informed about the corporation's activities, they are unable to exercise their rights of vote and proposal submissions effectively. This can indicate or lead to situations in which the interests of either the board or the executive are being served ahead of the interests of shareholders.

- *Ignorance regarding the corporation's activities.* Members on the board of directors are not required to understand the details and minutiae of corporate activity, because they are elected not to run the company but rather to govern how it is run. It is for this reason that one of the primary functions of the board is to appoint an able group of executives to run the corporation's activities. However, in order to monitor the decisions and actions of the executives effectively, members of the board must have a reasonable level of knowledge.

When board members lack the appropriate education and experience to understand the corporation's activities, they are increasingly susceptible to becoming dominated by the executive. Similar situations arise when the board does not remain properly informed about corporate activity, despite having the capacity to do so.

- *Unquestioning compliance with executive initiatives and decisions.* There are several instances in which the hierarchical structure of the corporation becomes reversed and the executive leads the board, instead of the board leading the executive. These situations can be very dangerous for investors as they are likely to result in an ignoring of their rights. An example of such an outcome would be inflated CEO compensation or severance packages.

- *An overbearing board.* The opposite of a board that subjugates itself to the will of the executive is one that impedes its ability to run the corporation. The board is charged with appointing a skilled and effective executive body to run the operations of the company. The board is then responsible for governing the executive to ensure that their actions are in the best interests of the company. Stepping beyond their role and attempting to run the corporation over the heads of the executive is a dangerous situation that not only disrupts the hierarchy of governance, but also risks damaging the financial success of the company.

- *Minority issues hijacking meetings.* When one or more board members dominate a director meeting with issues that do not represent the concerns of the shareholders or a significant portion of the board, they are diminishing the board's productivity and pushing their own interests.

Boards that are continually plagued by such problems demonstrate an inability to govern themselves and/or to control individual directors. This can be a symptom of a larger issue of board inadequacy and can represent the onset of future problems.

- *Ignoring shareholder proposals.* A corporation's board of directors is afforded discretionary privileges for including shareholder proposals on voting ballots and for implementing proposals that have achieved the majority of votes. A board that continually dismisses shareholder proposals can have a pattern of ignoring shareholder interests.

Indicators Relating to the Executive

Although it is unfair to paint all executives with the brush of scandal, it is true that most of the turn-of-the-millennium scandals were centered on the actions of executive members, particularly CEOs.

Because the executive is the group in charge of the corporation's operations, profiles of its members can offer insight into the overall financial and structural health of the corporation.

Some potential signs of danger that can be identified through the executive include:

- *Disregard for board policy.* One of the dangers with the greatest imminent risk is that of the rogue board. Evidence that the executive and CEO disregard the board's directions and policies are signs of a possible power imbalance between the board and the executive.

Further compounding the risk is a situation in which the policy violations occur without recourse. This shows not only that the executive is overstepping its authority, but also that the board is allowing the executive to do so.

The executive is charged with running the corporation, whereas the board is charged with governing it. While the executive serves the interests of the corporation, the board serves those of the investors. When these two competing interests coincide, synergies can be leveraged, but when they diverge, the will of the board and the interests of the shareholders ought to win.

In corporations where the hierarchy has been reversed, and the executive dominates the board, the needs of shareholders will not win.

- *Distrust or disdain toward the board.* Although it is not required that the executive have a love affair with the board of directors, it is imperative to the facilitation of business practices that the parties coexist amicably. Without mutual respect and trust, the executive and board will impede each other's productivity, at the expense of the company.

    Signs of distrust and disdain include the purposeful blocking of information and an unwillingness to communicate with the board or with specific board members. Creating such a barrier inhibits the board's ability to meet its fiduciary duties to the shareholders and jeopardizes its independent nature.

- *Infighting among executive members.* Just as executive members can exhibit disdain and distrust for board members, they can do the same for other executives as well. One common reason for such infighting is the promotion of one company member when another one or more were contenders for the same position. Another catalyst can be the establishment of dissenting factions within the executive over any number of issues.

Regardless of its cause, infighting in the executive poses as great of a potential threat as when it occurs between the executive and the board. In this case, however, the threat is not that the executive will dominate the board, but rather that their grudges will dominate their actions.

Corporations are meant to run toward the best interests of their owners, the shareholders. Executive infighting that detracts from that objective is a sign of potential danger, at present or in the future.

- *Conflicts of interest.* A more thorough discussion of conflicts of interest is presented elsewhere in this book, but here it is important to realize that conflicts of interest, whether actual or merely perceived, are a sign of potential danger. This is especially true when those potential conflicts are brought to the board or executive's attention and they are ignored or otherwise not addressed.

An executive member who is still functioning in his or her capacity within the corporation while experiencing an apparent conflict of interest is a potential liability. That conflict can create possible situations in which the member will act in the interests of others rather than those of the corporation.

It is also possible that an executive member with an apparent conflict of interest will harm the reputation of the corporation, in the process hindering growth and development. Finally, an unresolved conflict of interest can be indicative of a corporate structure in which the rights of the shareholders are not respected.

- *No changes to executive membership, despite a history of poor performance.* Board members or members of the executive can become entrenched. When this occurs, they will not be removed despite costs to corporate development and productivity, which harms the corporation as a whole and the investment of shareholders.

  Entrenchment is a serious concern that many organizations are working hard to prevent. Like situations in which the executive supersedes the board's power, entrenchment hijacks the objectives of the corporation and steals them from the shareholders, where they rightfully belong.

Indicators Relating to Shareholders

Shareholders are the owners of a corporation. As such, the behaviors of the shareholders are very tightly integrated with the company's success. Although they are not able to make direct decisions about the corporation's daily affairs, shareholders are able to set the overall tone for the corporation. There are several ways through which is achieved:

- *Poor attendance at annual shareholder meetings.* When the general shareholder population is apathetic toward corporate events, they allow minority or executive interests to dominate. Without alternative influence of a strong shareholder voice, minority shareholder issues can take over and may harm the company. Alternatively, when shareholders do not hold them accountable,

101

directors and executive members are able to fulfill their own interests rather than those of the shareholder.

- *Poor voter turnout for board elections and proposal votes.* When shareholders do not attend meetings, they have the ability to vote by proxy. However, should the majority of shareholders forgo their right to vote, they leave the decisions either to a small minority of shareholders or in the hands of the directors.

- *A minority voice hijacks shareholder issues.* As in any voting system, in corporations, a minority shareholder voice should be fairly represented and allowed neither to dominate nor go unheard. Although many minority issues are beneficial to the corporation or to the community, the issue should be judged not on its merit but rather on the volume of support that it receives. Shareholders are expected to have influence representative of their investment, and a minority issue with undue force violates this principle.

  Whether the issue is "good" or not, the ability of a minority voice to dominate the shareholder agenda is indicative of problems within the corporate structure. Such a situation can indicate, for example, shareholder apathy or a lack of organization in the shareholder meetings.

Indicators Relating to Finances

Aside from the factors relating to structure and people within the corporation, the company's financial health can also offer warning signs. Of course, it is important to remember that corporations with poor Corporate Governance records can have great financial success, and those with outstanding policies can end up bankrupt.

Instead of taking the financial situation as a definitive indicator, these factors should be considered as part of an overall evaluation:

- *Continually unmanaged debts.* A corporation that displays poor planning and management is giving a strong warning that there is an organizational problem. For example, this warning sign can indicate that the board does not have sufficient independence to effectively regulate and appoint a successful executive.

- *Depletion of reserve funds without viable plans for rebuilding.* Again, a situation such as this indicates poor planning and financial management on the part of the executive. It also demonstrates that the board is unable or unwilling to monitor its own actions in a meaningful way. When a long-standing problem such as this exists, shareholders should be concerned about board or executive entrenchment, deep-rooted corruption, or a lack of board independence.

- *Failure to meet targeted performance ranks.* Targeted performance ranks are subjective, and failure to meet the projections one year should not be taken as an accurate sign of trouble. However, a company that continues to fail to meet its targets is likely experiencing financial problems. Such an ongoing problem can also indicate stunted growth and development. At the very least, when a corporation continually fails to meet its projections, the public and its shareholders should ask why.

- *Inaccurate financial reports.* Not all financial reporting errors are indicative of corruption. However, a long history of such errors does demonstrate that the corporation is having internal challenges. This is especially true given compliance regulations like the Sarbanes-Oxley (SOX) Act, which should minimize the occurrence of accounting and financial reporting errors. Given the controls and procedures required under SOX, there are few excuses for continual "honest" mistakes. Instead, it is fair to assume that a string of inaccurate financial reports is the result of poor management, an ineffective board, or a failure within the corporation's accounting and/or internal control systems.

- *Continual difficulty complying with SEC regulations.* The Securities and Exchange Commission (SEC) governs corporations and works to ensure that shareholders receive accurate and timely information. When a company fails to comply with an SEC regulation, its shareholders are likely left without important information. A pattern of compliance failures may indicate a problem at the level of filing the SEC paperwork, but it can also be hiding a deeper issue of corruption or mismanagement.

- *Difficulty complying with the requirements of SOX.* SOX and the Public Company Accounting Oversight Board (PCAOB) govern the auditing practices within corporations. SOX is tightly linked to the role of the SEC, and several principles overlap. As with the SEC, failure to comply with the PCAOB Auditing Standards and SOX can indicate a structural problem in the corporation or even the presence of corruption. However, as the act is still relatively new, compliance issues at this point can still be linked to difficulties understanding and interpreting it.

Conclusion

When corporations get into trouble with the law or other regulatory organizations, it is easy to blame the greed of an individual or the malice of a group. Taking this attitude does not help to combat the problem of corporate crime, however, because it essentially leaves the occurrence up to chance: bad luck in investing in the wrong company or in appointing a "bad apple" CEO.

An alternative approach is to try to rectify the situations from which the corruption arises in order to facilitate ethical corporate cultures and transparent dealings. This is an approach that is arguably more desirable because it empowers the individual to create change rather than simply to accept risk.

The first step toward changing a potentially dangerous situation within a corporation is to clearly identify the situation. This chapter has listed situations that could indicate risk of corruption and identified some of the warning signs of corporate problems. Although on their own, few of these issues may be definitive indicators, taken as a group, they can provide strong warning signs of danger.

It is very rare that a corporation will collapse without exhibiting at least one of these indicators. Recognizing them can help stakeholders at all levels of the corporation protect themselves and the integrity of the company as a whole.

Summary

- An indicator of trouble is not a definitive sign that there is a problem.
- Board-related indicators include a lack of independence, failure to meet the needs of shareholders, and a poor relationship with the executive.

- Executive-related indicators include a poor relationship with the board, entrenchment, and poor management decisions.

- Shareholder-related indicators include displays of apathy and the dominance of minority issues.

- Finance-related indicators include displays of poor planning, such as unmanaged debt, and continual disregard for governing regulations.

CHAPTER 8

Changes Made Through Corporate Governance

After reading this chapter, you will

- Understand areas recommended for Corporate Governance attention
- Understand whistle-blowing procedures
- Understand the value codes of ethics
- Understand performance evaluations
- Understand the director election process

When a company starts to evaluate and revise its governance strategies, the first requirement is that the corporation's structure facilitates change. This means that the board and the executive must be organized in a manner conducive to establishing new guidelines and must not be burdened by entrenchment.

As the corporation begins moving toward good Corporate Governance, some of the areas it will address include the establishment of whistle-blowing procedures and protection, the creation of one or more ethics codes, restructuring of board and executive evaluation and compensation strategies, and assessment of the director nomination and election process.

Whistle-blower Procedures

The term "whistle-blowing" applies to the actions of any company member who exposes a perceived wrongdoing that is occurring within the organization.

Importance of the Whistle-blower

Two types of impressions surround whistle-blowing. On one hand, there are those who value whistle-blowers and view them as brave people trying to combat corruption and unethical behavior. On the other hand, some still view whistle-blowers with contempt and consider them traitors to their company or colleagues.

There is no reason why this negative view of whistle-blowers should prevail. When conducted properly and with integrity, whistle-blower activities provide a valuable service to the company as well as to the general public.

It is the position of the Securities and Exchange Commission (SEC) and other governing bodies that those within the company are the most likely to identify problems. This is why whistle-blower rights are becoming an important topic; without protection, whistle-blowers are less likely to come forward, and problems are more likely to remain undetected.

Protecting the Rights of Whistle-blowers

The rights of whistle-blowers within a company publicly traded on a U.S. market are protected by the Sarbanes-Oxley (SOX) Act. The provisions of the act protect whistle-blowers by outlining actions that would be considered prohibited retribution. This section of the act also provides protection by offering specific penalties that may be implemented should whistle-blowers suffer from retribution as a direct result of their reporting activities.

Establishing Policies

SOX requires that corporations establish their own internal policies and procedures to facilitate whistle-blowing activities and prevent unfair retribution. Key components of these policies will be the inclusion of privacy provisions, processes for reporting, strategies for investigating reports, and, in some cases, the establishment of a compliance officer or committee.

Duties of the Whistle-blower

Just as the company should be governed by whistle-blowing policies, so should whistle-blowers follow a code of conduct.

Generally speaking, whistle-blowers are expected to move through appropriate channels within their company before going public with their concerns. In other words, after detecting a problem, the company member will seek an internal solution before involving outside organizations.

Whistle-blowers are also expected to conduct themselves with a strong sense of honesty and integrity. Their allegations should be based on evidence and stem from a reasonable belief that a problem is occurring.

Educating Employees

In order for a whistle-blowing policy to be effective, company members must be informed and educated about the rights and duties of whistle-blowers. An employee education program could include the publishing of a formal written code and ethics workshops that discuss whistle-blowing. Most important, employees need to understand the avenues available to them should they have a concern to report.

IN THE REAL WORLD

Whistle-blowers of the Early 2000s

As the public watched Enron, Tyco, WorldCom, and other corporations marred by scandal, they also witnessed the deification of the whistle-blowers who sounded the alarms.

Sherron Watkins

The 2001 Enron scandal is strongly linked to the company's former vice president, Sherron Watkins, who is credited with exposing the corruption. Although she was acclaimed by *Time* magazine in 2002 as one of the Persons of the Year, Watkins's label of whistle-blower has also been publicly contested.

The argument centers on the infamous whistle-blowing e-mail Watkins sent to Enron chairman Kenneth Lay in August 2001. This e-mail outlined the accounting irregularities that Watkins suspected. When the e-mail was released to the public five months later, it served as the whistle-blowing vehicle.

Vital to evaluating Watkins's actions is the fact that Lay himself was later implicated in the scandal. Those who argue that Watkins is not a true whistle-blower believe that she should have alerted the public immediately and directly. Conversely, others assert that in bringing the issues to Lay's attention first, Watkins was moving though the appropriate channels to rectify the problem.

Cynthia Cooper

Similar to Sherron Watkins's situation (and a *Time* Person of the Year in 2002), Cynthia Cooper, WorldCom's whistle-blower, has also been questioned about how long it took her to release the information. Cooper, the Vice President of Internal Audit at World-Com, uncovered $3.9 billion in inflated profits. Although she reported her findings to the corporation's board of directors, she did not make the information public until seven months later.

Code of Ethics

The establishment of a code of ethics is not a new concept within companies. It is something that most corporations implemented at their inception but have not revisited in several years. A corporation's code of ethics should establish guidelines and expectations for company members so that they can understand what issues they must consider in their actions and decisions. An ethics code is valuable in the sense that it removes the question of whether an action is tolerable to the corporation or not and reduces the ambiguity that can arise from unclear and unwritten guidelines.

By providing their members with clear and complete ethics codes, corporations take away the guesswork and ensure that all directors, executives, and employees understand their roles.

Principles of the Code

In general, a corporation's code of ethics will include guidelines for dealing with financial records, expectations for compliance with laws and regulations, procedures for identifying and eliminating conflicts of interest, an explanation of the company's code of confidentiality and its enforcement, and strategies for the promotion of an ethical environment within the company.

Setting an Example

The establishment of an ethical environment within a corporation requires the cooperation of all company members. However, it is particularly important that members of management set the example for all other employees.

If those who run the corporation do not respect or enforce the company's code of ethics, then it is very difficult to foster a high standard at lower levels. Furthermore, corruption at high levels often carries greater risks for the company, making management's compliance a priority.

Code Establishment

The shape that a corporation's code of ethics will take varies depending on the unique structure of the company. Where one company may find that one code will suffice, others may choose to establish separate codes for various regions and levels within the company. For example, within an international corporation, the multiple-code strategy for the various geographic regions may be the best choice. This is because employees can face different ethical situations depending on a country's political and social circumstances. Similarly, a code of ethics is often established specifically for executive management to reflect their unique ethical concerns.

Code Enforcement and Evaluation

Many corporations opt to establish a special committee within the board of directors to deal specifically with ethics. This committee is responsible for the establishment, evaluation, and enforcement of the code of ethics.

It is the role of the ethics committee not only to establish the code, but also to reevaluate and revise it at regular intervals. This exercise is important because as the circumstances of the company and society evolve, the ethical dilemmas faced by employees will change. For example, consider a code of ethics that was written in the early 1980s. Although many principles within the code will still apply, it will likely make no mention of the Internet or any ethical situations that arise as a result.

The code of ethics itself should direct the enforcement of its principles. During its establishment, writers of the code must consider fair and reasonable consequences for ethical violations.

Performance Evaluations

Board and executive evaluation is vital to a healthy corporation. When a corporation is running properly, the board of directors should be able to identify problems among its own members as well as those of the executive. After identifying these issues, the board takes measures to remove or rectify the problem, thus ensuring that the corporate body remains as productive and effective as possible.

Corporate Governance concerns often focus on board and executive evaluation. Regarding the board of directors, there is concern that the board cannot evaluate itself and its members objectively. However, when the board of directors is not sufficiently independent, one of the first worries is that it will be unable to evaluate the executive objectively.

The principal preventive measure is to ensure that the board is independent and able to govern the executive effectively. Additional strategies to ensure objective evaluation include consideration of external evaluations, such as those provided by financial institutions, implementation of set terms of service, and the prohibition of automatic renomination of incumbent directors.

Compensation Packages

Along with evaluation, compensation packages of the board and executive are also a major issue in Corporate Governance. While the compensation levels for board members are outlined in the corporation's bylaws, the board has the power to make amendments.

Establishing and evaluating compensation packages is the job of the board's compensation committee. It is because of its ability to determine the allocation of significant company resources that the compensation committee must be independent from undue influence by the executive or other board members.

IN THE REAL WORLD

The Overpaid Chief Executive Officer

The media frequently reports on the large salaries earned by some chief executive officers (CEOs); a favorite technique is to speak in terms of thousands of dollars per minute. Although it is true that some CEOs are likely overpaid, this is not necessarily the norm.

As with all other professions, salaries for CEOs largely depend on the corporation that they run. Corporations come in all sizes and industries, and have varying levels of success within those industries. The wide salary range actually earned by CEOs reflects this variety, and most salaries are not nearly as impressive as the ones the media reports.

Furthermore, even when a CEO's salary appears to be astronomically large, it is not necessarily true that the value is unwarranted. According to one argument, corporations benefit from high CEO salaries because those salaries allow them to recruit the best prospects.

Director Elections

Looking back at our discussion of board entrenchment and its dangers, we can see that board elections are a vital component of a healthy Corporate Governance structure. The board is the shareholder representative, and must therefore truly represent the wishes of the majority of shareholders.

As shown in Exhibit 8.1, issues that threaten this principle include:

- Hostile takeovers

- Secretive nomination practices

- Pressures that eliminate autonomous voting practices

A corporation interested in fostering good Corporate Governance practices will make efforts to ensure that the nomination and voting procedures are fair and representative. Some techniques used to protect the integrity of board election include:

- *Transparent nomination procedure.* Generally speaking, the nomination committee of the board of directors is responsible for putting forward nominees for election. In many situations, board members, other company members, shareholders, and outside stakeholders select the individuals who are recommended for nomination.

   After collecting the recommendations, the nomination committee evaluates each candidate and then submits a final list to the voting shareholders for election.

   Several circumstances threaten the nomination procedure; one occurs when the board does not provide shareholders with adequate information on which to base their votes. Another circumstance involves the automatic nomination of incumbent directors.

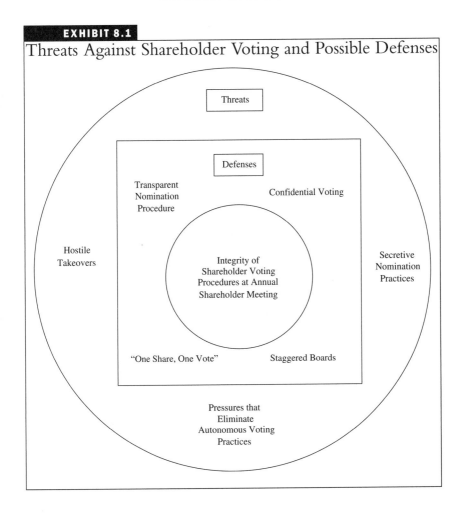

EXHIBIT 8.1

Threats Against Shareholder Voting and Possible Defenses

Threats

Defenses

Transparent Nomination Procedure

Confidential Voting

Hostile Takeovers

Integrity of Shareholder Voting Procedures at Annual Shareholder Meeting

Secretive Nomination Practices

"One Share, One Vote"

Staggered Boards

Pressures that Eliminate Autonomous Voting Practices

Even in situations where directors have been valuable members of the board, their nomination should not be automatic. A better alternative would be that incumbent directors are evaluated in the same manner as all other recommended nominees. This will ensure that the shareholders remain confident that the nominee list is comprised only of the best possible candidates.

- *Confidential and representative voting.* As with any election, the opinions of the voters are truly represented only when they are able to vote in confidence and when their votes are fairly weighed. In terms of the corporation, representative voting usually entails the "one share, one vote" principle, whereby each shareholder's vote counts according to the weight of his or her ownership in the corporation.

- *Staggered boards.* A staggered board is one in which the directors' terms will end over a period of time, rather than in the same year. One benefit of the staggered board structure is that it helps slow down, and sometimes prevent, the occurrence of hostile takeovers. This is because the incoming directors are able to fill only a certain number of seats in any given election, meaning they have to wait several years before gaining the majority.

Conclusion

Good Corporate Governance is based on creating and facilitating changes toward a more effective operation and a greater respect for shareholder rights. This chapter has discussed several of the major changes that improve a company's Corporate Governance practices, including whistle-blower protection, the fostering of an ethical environment, and the creation of stronger board policies in terms of evaluations, compensation, and nominations.

Essentially, a corporation cannot hope to establish a strong record of good Corporate Governance until it has in place not only the policies but also the framework for their enforcement.

Summary

- Whistle-blowers are those who expose potential problems with a company's actions or policies.

- Establishing an effective policy to facilitate whistle-blowing means creating a system for reporting concerns, actively protecting the rights of whistle-blowers, and educating company members about whistle-blower responsibilities.

- A corporation's code of ethics should reflect the company's unique structure to ensure that the code will be effective. This can mean the establishment of multiple codes for different regions and levels within the company.

- The board of directors must have sufficient independence in order to objectively fulfill its role of evaluating the executive and itself.

- Board independence is also a factor in the board's ability to objectively set compensation packages for its members and members of the executive.

CHAPTER 9

Regulations and Strategies for Corporate Governance

After reading this chapter, you will be able to

- Understand the significance of the Sarbanes-Oxley Act
- Understand the importance of Securities and Exchange Commission proxy reform
- Understand the role of the Organization of Economic Co-operation and Development
- Understand the Balanced Scorecard

The way that a company is run determines the level of confidence that its shareholders and other stakeholders will have in it. A company with a strong performance history will garner more trust and in turn will likely reap financial benefits. Investors will be more likely to buy stock, the company will have an easier time wooing top executives, and partnerships will be quicker to form.

There is another consideration, however, that goes beyond the individual company; that is the consideration of the market as a whole. A marketplace in which most, or all, companies have a strong image will benefit as the individual corporation does, but in an aggregate manner.

The companies within this market will have greater trust from their shareholders and a higher investment base on which to build their organizations. Similarly, these companies will also require fewer regulations and therefore enjoy greater freedom.

Unfortunately, it takes only a small number of highly publicized, poorly run companies to taint an entire market. Suddenly all corporations, even those already strongly run, face the same investor suspicion, the same strict regulations, and the same damaged economy.

It is because of this "one bad apple" effect that so many organizations and systems have been established to help guide corporations toward practices of good Corporate Governance: When one corporation fails, it is not only that one that suffers.

Sarbanes-Oxley Act

The Sarbanes-Oxley (SOX) Act was passed in 2002 with the intention of protecting investors and establishing guidelines for financial reporting. Investors and other interested parties use a corporation's financial records and related information as a method of evaluating the corporation.

When the information is incomplete or otherwise misrepresentative, those who rely on the information are deceived. Consequently, their ability to make sound decisions will be impaired. The effects of false information can be as dire for accidental misrepresentation as they can for purposeful deception. It is for this reason that effective controls against both error and corruption are vital.

In the most basic terms, SOX requires that corporate executives—chief executive officers (CEOs) and chief financial officers (CFOs)—take responsibility for the accuracy of their corporations' financial records and for the processes of releasing complete information to shareholders. These regulations are legally binding for publicly listed businesses that are domestic to the United States and foreign companies traded on U.S. stock exchanges.

Although geared specifically toward the structures of U.S. corporations, SOX is becoming a benchmark standard in accounting best principles. With minor adjustments, its guidelines can be applied not only internationally but also to nonpublic organizations.

TIPS AND TECHNIQUES

Applying the Key Principles of SOX to All Organizations

The Sarbanes-Oxley Act was established as a legally binding code of regulations for publicly traded corporations on the U.S. markets. In terms of Corporate Governance, this act can be considered a document of accounting best principles. Its principles are applicable to achieving good Corporate Governance policies in all organizations.

The three integral principles of SOX are integrity, reliability, and accountability. Looking into these principles a little deeper demonstrates that they reflect Corporate Governance not simply in terms of accounting practices but as overall guiding principles.

- *Integrity.* The SOX principle of integrity refers to the completeness of the financial records; it does not refer to a personality characteristic. Investors use a corporation's financial information to obtain a picture of the company's financial health. Should the information be incomplete, investors will not have a representative image of the company's situation. For this reason, SOX provides guidelines on the types of relevant information that must be disclosed.

  Corporations that seek to meet the needs of their shareholders and sustain strong public images must be concerned with fostering integrity within all areas of the company. "Integrity of individuals" means the creation of and adherence to codes of ethics that promote high moral and professional standards. In addition, "institutional integrity" means complete and secure accounting principles, informational processes, and communication with shareholders.

  A corporation that embraces the principle of integrity will have made every effort to identify potential weakness that could be exploited for corrupt behavior.

- *Reliability.* As a principle of SOX, "reliability" is the concept of accurate information. The public and investors need to be able to trust that the information with which they are presented is correct. As mentioned, honest errors can create as much damage as purposeful deceits. SOX seeks to limit both forms of misrepresentation by requiring that companies establish controls for the protection of their financial information and its accuracy.

Reliability in Corporate Governance practices takes the concept a step further, expecting reliability at all levels of communication with shareholders. It expects that board members will be reliable in the fulfilling of their fiduciary duties to shareholders.

Reliable Corporate Governance practices also extend to communications outside of financial reporting. A corporation that is reliable will provide accurate and reliable information to shareholders regarding policy changes, director nominations, and all other topics that shareholders require updates on.

- *Accountability*. When looking at SOX, *accountability* refers to the principle that within the corporation, someone must be held accountable for the establishment of controls and the consequences should those controls fail. Although SOX does provide some direction for board members, it is the CEO and CFO of the corporation who shoulder the responsibility of complying with SOX.

  In terms of Corporate Governance, however, accountability falls onto the directors of the board. As the corporate members with fiduciary duties to the shareholders, the board is ultimately accountable when it fails to sufficiently consider the interests of shareholders.

Within SOX, two sections have received the most attention: Sections 302 and 404. Section 302 mandates that the CEO and CFO design systems to ensure that they receive all important information about their company. Furthermore, the CEO and CFO must certify that they are accountable for the creation of these systems and their subsequent success or failure. The purpose of this section is to ensure that the CEO and CFO are able to certify the accuracy of all financial information issued by the company.

Section 404 deals with the creation of controls to ensure that the financial records are accurate. Compliance with Section 404 requires companies to evaluate the security of their current systems and create protections that would prevent false information from being released.

Put another way, SOX Section 404 mandates the creation of controls to ensure that financial records are accurate and complete; SOX Section 302 mandates the creation of controls to ensure that the CEO and CFO are able to accept accountability for the accuracy of those records.

Securities and Exchange Commission Regulations for Shareholder Proposals

We have consistently discussed the importance of shareholder activity throughout this book, but it is worth mentioning again. Shareholders, as the owners of corporations, have a material interest in the company's events and status, and should therefore be able and willing to participate actively.

In most situations, shareholder participation occurs through reading quarterly reports, attending shareholder meetings, and voting. Shareholders are also able to offer their own proposals and establish advocacy committees to increase their involvement.

The 1934 Securities Exchange Act governs the process by which shareholders are able to submit proposals. This process is outlined in Regulation 14a-8. According to the 1998 amended version of the section, shareholders are eligible to submit proposals if they have held 1% of the company's voting stock for a term of one year or more. The guidelines also limit shareholders to one proposal per meeting.

Of course, these guidelines only regulate the submission of proposals; it is up to the board to determine if a proposal will be put forward for vote. Even if the board is unable to exclude a proposal, it can still formally recommend that shareholders vote against it. Directors are also able to choose whether to act on a shareholder proposal that has been agreed to by the majority.

TIPS AND TECHNIQUES

Meeting Proposal Requirements

One of the rights of a shareholder is to be involved in the corporation's activities through the submission of proposals. After submission, these proposals are reviewed by the board of directors, who determine if they will be put to the shareholders for voting.

There are a number of reasons why the board will terminate a proposal before allowing shareholders to vote on it. Many of these reasons relate to the technical requirements of a proposal. Shareholders will have a greater chance of seeing their proposal included in the company's proxy statement if they abide by those regulations.

Although adhering to these requirements does not guarantee inclusion, failure to do so does guarantee exclusion. That is why it is important that shareholder proposals meet these regulations:

- The shareholder submitting the proposal must own 1% of the company's shares at the time of submission and have owned that stock for at least one year.
- The submitting shareholder must continue to own at least 1% of the company's shares through the date on which the proposal is voted on.

Organization for Economic Co-Operation and Development

The Organization for Economic Co-operation and Development (OECD) offers membership for 30 countries and has a relationship with over 70 others. Although perhaps best known for its work with public corporations and Corporate Governance, the OECD is involved with other economic areas, including nongovernmental organizations.

The role played by the OECD is one of research and guidance. The organization facilitates policy discussion, generates statistics, and publishes guidelines, such as its *Principles of Corporate Governance*.

In 1999, the OECD released the first edition of the *OECD Principles of Corporate Governance*.[1] Although geared toward the organization's 30 member countries, this document has also served as a global guide for Corporate Governance efforts.

Recent revisions to the principles have considered the changing corporate culture, the growth of the global economy, and highly publicized accounting scandals. Although these guidelines do provide specific recommendations and advice, they are not necessarily designed for direct implementation into a corporate body.

Instead, these principles have been created to serve as a starting point, a set of regulations that evens the playing field so that all countries start on the same page with basic concepts of Corporate Governance. The countries are then left to develop their own policies and regulations that meet these requirements, but in a manner representative of their unique corporate and economic structures.

The principles themselves focus on Corporate Governance by breaking it into five areas: basic framework, shareholder rights, stakeholder considerations, transparency, and board responsibilities.

1. *Framework.* The OECD is a vocal advocate of establishing a foundational framework for Corporate Governance. This framework should facilitate and coordinate Corporate Governance efforts as well as be cognizant of all relevant laws and regulations.

2. *Shareholder rights.* Shareholders are in the unique position of having put up the capital for the company but not having direct control over how it is run. This means that their investment in the company must be protected, and their trust in the system cannot be abused. This is a key focus of Corporate Governance.

3. *Stakeholder considerations.* Although stakeholders are not given equal treatment in all corporate frameworks, the OECD does support fair treatment and consideration of all company stakeholders.

4. *Transparency.* In sustaining the rights of the shareholders, it is important that corporations facilitate truthful disclosure of

information and sufficient transparency in their processes. Doing so allows shareholders and others with interest in the companies to obtain an accurate picture of their activities and financial situation.

5. *Responsibilities of the board.* As the shareholder's representative within the corporation, the OECD recognizes its vital role in corporate governance. Specifically, the board is responsible for monitoring the actions of the executive and management, as well as evaluating itself in terms of accountability to the corporations and the shareholders.

IN THE REAL WORLD

Member Countries
of the OECD

The Organization of Economic Co-operation and Development (OECD) is the creator of the *OECD Principles of Corporate Governance,* the definitive guide for its member countries and many others. OECD membership has grown consistently since the early 1960s and now includes 30 countries. These countries and their ratification dates are:

Australia	June 7, 1971
Austria	September 29, 1961
Belgium	September 13, 1961
Canada	April 10, 1961
Czech Republic	December 21, 1995
Denmark	May 30, 1961
Finland	January 28, 1969
France	August 7, 1961
Germany	September 27, 1961

IN THE REAL WORLD (CONTINUED)

Greece	September 27, 1961
Hungary	May 7, 1996
Iceland	June 5, 1961
Ireland	August 17, 1961
Italy	March 29, 1962
Japan	April 28, 1964
Korea	December 12, 1996
Luxembourg	December 7, 1961
Mexico	May 18, 1994
Netherlands	November 13, 1961
New Zealand	May 29, 1973
Norway	July 4, 1961
Poland	November 22, 1996
Portugal	August 4, 1961
Slovak Republic	December 14, 2000
Spain	August 3, 1961
Sweden	September 28, 1961
Switzerland	September 28, 1961
Turkey	August 2, 1961
United Kingdom	May 2, 1961
United States	April 12, 1961

Source: Organization for Economic Co-operation and Development, "Ratification of the Convention on the OECD," OECD Database, www.oecd.org.

*C*adbury Report

The Cadbury Commission's *Financial Aspects of Corporate Governance*, more commonly known as the *Cadbury Report*, has made a strong contribution to the process of Corporate Governance in the United Kingdom and has influenced Corporate Governance efforts around the world.

Included in the report is a commendation for the *Code of Best Boardroom Practice*. Compliance with this code is a requirement for all companies listed on the London Stock Exchange; however, this compliance is based on the "if not, why not?" concept. This means that those corporations that do not comply with one or more sections of the *Code of Best Boardroom Practice* must offer an explanation for their noncompliance.

In general, the *Cadbury Report* focuses on the importance of establishing a strong and independent board of directors. One of the key components of doing so is to separate the roles of the board chairperson and the CEO.

It has become increasingly accepted that the role of the CEO and the chair of the board should be held by two individuals rather than one combined. The principle reasoning for this is that having one person function as both CEO and chair creates a conflict of interest and inhibits the board's ability to evaluate the executive objectively.

Although the separation of these two positions is recommended by the *Cadbury Report* and most other respected Corporate Governance documents, not all companies have embraced the concept. This situation is slowly changing, however, and it is likely that a time will come in which combining the roles will be taboo.

Balanced Scorecard

The Balanced Scorecard strategy was developed to simplify and streamline the way in which a corporate executive thinks about the corporation's priorities and obligations. In a sense, the Scorecard is meant to provide the big-picture approach so that the executive does not lose sight of the goals when focusing on the details.

A further benefit of the Scorecard is that it provides a concrete strategy for evaluating intangible, nonfinancial objectives. While it has long been advisable that all executives create a Scorecard or adopt a similar approach, it is now becoming clear that the strategy is also effective for boards.

There are four components of a Balanced Scorecard:

1. *Financial.* The financial portion of the Scorecard provides discussion of the cost-revenue aspects of the project. This section contains the financial figures for the profitability of the strategy as well as the potential for growth, costs per unit, and share value impact.

2. *Customer.* The customer portion of the Scorecard links the customer and market activity to the financial success of the strategy.

3. *Organization.* The organization portion of the Scorecard recognizes the actions that will have to occur on the part of the corporation in order to generate the market activity that will support the financial outcome.

4. *Development.* Finally, the development portion of the Scorecard links the internal development that will be required to support the organization's efforts. For example, this section may include personnel expansions.

Good Corporate Governance Components

Corporations with strong histories of good Corporate Governance take time to build; they do not happen overnight. One of the key factors in establishing good Corporate Governance practices within a company is to prepare. The committee or individual in charge of establishing such practices needs to be educated about important issues and concepts; also, the committee or person must take an inventory of the company.

Good Corporate Governance is built on the foundation of a strong corporate culture. If the company and its members are not behind the action, implementing Corporate Governance practices will be an uphill struggle. That is why it is important that companies evaluate their internal structure and culture to determine if they are ready for Corporate Governance. Here is a list of indicators that a corporation is ready for Corporate Governance success. If these indicators are weak or missing, the corporation should take immediate steps to remedy the situation as part of its initial good Corporate Governance efforts. (See Exhibit 9.1.)

- *Strong ethical culture within the company.* Without strong ethics in the corporation and among its members, the company will not be able to establish effective Corporate Governance principles. In most circumstances, the board of directors will establish an ethics committee to oversee the establishment and enforcement of the code of ethics.

  Having a code of ethics is a good start, but it is not enough. The code will be effective only if all company members know it, understand it, and abide by it. This means that the company needs to invest not only in the development of the code but also in the education of all company members.

  In some circumstances it is advisable for the company to establish different codes for the various levels of the corporation. Each role within the company, whether it is board member,

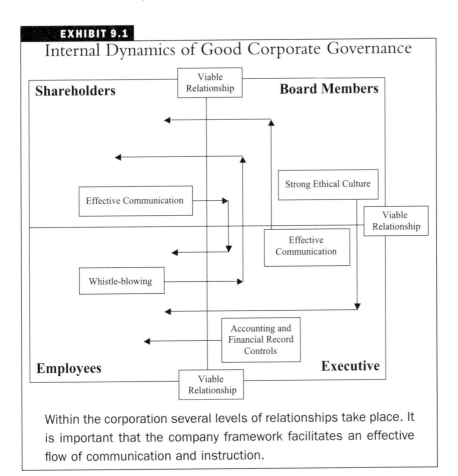

EXHIBIT 9.1

Internal Dynamics of Good Corporate Governance

Within the corporation several levels of relationships take place. It is important that the company framework facilitates an effective flow of communication and instruction.

management, or employee, has distinct needs for ethical guidance.

- *Effective communication among shareholders, board members, and the executive.* Good Corporate Governance requires that the shareholders are informed of the corporation's activities so that they can monitor their investment effectively. Companies where the board does not communicate regularly with the shareholders must first remedy this situation and open the lines of communication.

Similarly, the board of directors must receive accurate and timely information about the corporation's activities and the decisions of the executive members. Without this level of communication, the board will not be able to effectively monitor the actions and decisions of the executive.

In evaluating the efficacy of a company's Corporate Governance, it is important to consider the communication avenues because where the lines of communication end, Corporate Governance ends as well.

- *Viable relationship among all top-level groups and committees.* We have all heard that business is not personal, but personal relationships sometimes create business boundaries. If company members work toward their own agenda rather than that of the company, they are impeding efforts toward good Corporate Governance.

  In the process of evaluating a corporation's culture, one key component is identifying any barriers within the company. This will mean looking closely at the relationships between board members and the various committees to identify any breakdowns in the communication or hints of self-interest.

  Another component will be to assess the relationship between the executive and the board. A healthy relationship between directors and management is one in which the executive defers to the board's authority, but the board allows the executive freedom to run the company effectively.

- *Effective whistle-blowing policies and protections in place.* Several corporations implicated for accounting fraud during the scandals of the 1990s and early 2000s were exposed by whistle-blowers from within the company. The Securities and Exchange Commission (SEC) and other organizations understand that no matter how much information they gain about a company, they will never know as much as those on the inside.

For this reason, internal policies that facilitate whistle-blowing activities and protect individuals in the aftermath are major components of Corporate Governance policies. The board of directors should establish policies by which whistle-blowers can report their information and their privacy is maintained.

These same policies should clearly outline the manner in which whistle-blowers will be protected from recrimination. This is a vital component of ensuring that those with information will feel secure in disclosing it.

- *Well-established controls for accurate accounting and financial reporting.* Although the concept of Corporate Governance is growing beyond the idea of accuracy in accounting practices for stockholder protection, this value will always remain a central component. No company that has insufficient or ineffective controls to protect the integrity of its financial records will be able to implement good Corporate Governance practices successfully. The SEC, Public Company Accounting Oversight Board, and SOX are all major players in directing companies on how to regulate their flow of data and finances in a secure manner.

Past events have made it all too clear that gaps in accounting practices can be exploited to the gain of some and the severe loss of others. By auditing their flow of financial information and SOX compliance efforts, companies will gain a feel for how well their internal controls are functioning.

Components of a General Ethics Code

One of the first Corporate Governance efforts that companies should make is the establishment of a code of ethics. Depending on the size and nature of the corporation, one or more codes will be required. In many instances, a committee of ethics will be established among board members. This committee will not only establish the code, but will also govern its implementation and oversee any violations.

Although all corporations will have their own unique requirements for the code, most companies will find general components relevant. Specifically, a strong code of ethics will deal with matters related to these subjects:

- Expectation that executive and board members will lead by example; exemplifying ethical behavior and tolerating nothing less in their peers and subordinates
- Strategies of ethical training for all company members that include a schedule for updating their education and offering regular reminders
- Processes to facilitate whistle-blowing and protect those who come forward from retribution
- System for reviewing the code, its efficacy, and the company's overall compliance
- Standards expected from outside contractors, especially those dealing with law and accounting
- Elimination of situations that could create possible conflicts of interest

Conclusion

Corporations are not isolated entities whose actions affect no one but themselves. Instead, they are embedded within a society and within an industry. This means that the actions of one company can influence the general perception of corporations in society, either in a positive or negative way.

In the past we have seen plenty of examples of how the actions of one corporation mar the public's opinion of corporations as a whole. People in general, and astute investors in particular, are very wary of this risk. Damage their trust enough times and they will stop offering it.

Internationally speaking, a plethora of principles and guides recommend Corporate Governance best practices. This chapter has elaborated on some of those that are most likely to be encountered by U.S. companies and their subsidiaries.

As one of the newest members of the Corporate Governance landscape, SOX is specially geared toward the establishment of sound and reliable accounting practices within corporations traded on U.S. exchanges. The principles of SOX are universally applicable, however, and can serve as a strong foundation for enhancing Corporate Governance practices in all organizations.

Another U.S. pillar of Corporate Governance is the SEC. Discussion of the SEC in this chapter has been limited to its regulations of shareholder proposal protocol.

As an international organization, the OECD works to help nations establish functioning regulations to foster good Corporate Governance practices in their corporations. The OECD *Principles of Corporate Governance* has been a long-standing benchmark for Corporate Governance principles and continues to serve as a normative basis.

Finally, the *Cadbury Report* is one of the United Kingdom's contributions to the Corporate Governance conversation. The report, which was commissioned by the London Stock Exchange, elucidates the *Code of Best Boardroom Practice* and strongly advocates board independence.

This chapter ends with a collective summary of the Corporate Governance best practices from around world. This information is not only a learning reference but also a practical tool to aid in the enhancement of Corporate Governance policies and practices.

Summary

- SOX is legislation that requires enhanced accounting controls and practices for all companies traded on U.S. markets, both domestic and foreign.

- SOX deals with accuracy, reliability, and accountability in terms of a corporation's financial reporting practices.

- Stockholders wishing to submit proposals for voting at a corporation's annual shareholder meeting must meet specific regulations that are governed by the SEC.

- The OECD created the *OECD Principles of Corporate Governance* as an international benchmark to help facilitate efforts of various nations to establish Corporate Governance regulations.

- The *OECD Principles of Corporate Governance* focus on the Corporate Governance framework, shareholder rights, stakeholder considerations, transparency, and board responsibilities.

- The London Stock Exchange commissioned a report, which is now commonly known as the *Cadbury Report*. This report is a strong advocate of best boardroom practices including board independence.

Note

1. Fianna Jesover and Grant Kirkpatrick, *The Revised OECD Principles of Corporate Governance and Their Relevance to Non-OECD Countries* (Organization for Economic Co-operation and Development, 1999).

PART FOUR

International Perspective

CHAPTER 10

International Corporate Governance

After reading this chapter, you will be able to

- Understand that variations exist among the corporations of different countries
- Understand the concept of the international corporation
- Understand the influence of international investors
- Understand the role of the Global Corporate Governance Forum

Although this book's principal focus has been Corporate Governance and the U.S. corporation, no picture can be complete without taking a look at the international perspective.

In today's economy, the concept of the borderless corporation is becoming increasingly ubiquitous. There are few restrictions placed on investors who would like to purchase shares in international companies. There is also a strong trend toward the globalization of markets in which corporations themselves do not operate within confined borders but hold subsidiaries in several countries.

The international marketplace creates very specific complications for the establishment of good Corporate Governance practices. As previously discussed, corporations and their structure are unique to the countries in which they are situated. Their structures and practices have evolved from the unique political and social landscapes in which they are embedded.

This is the primary reason why Corporate Governance best practices are designed as guides to be adapted for specific circumstances rather than uniform implementation. Complications arise when companies are established in several unique marketplaces or when partnerships are created across international borders.

In these situations the corporation may find it difficult to create a companywide set of policies, since not every subsidiary will fit the bill. This chapter offers an introduction into these concepts and complexities.

Corporations Around the World

A common theme discussed throughout this book is the concept of corporations as entities that have evolved from the unique circumstances of their countries. Earlier chapters have illustrated that political, social, and economic landscapes work together with historical events to shape the corporate structures that are apparent within each region. Some broad categories of widely recognized models of Corporate Governance are:

- *U.S. corporate model.* The hallmark of the U.S. corporate model is the premium that it places on the interests of the shareholders.

- *Stakeholder model.* In the United Kingdom and Japan, a model similar to the U.S. one exists. However, in the stakeholder model, the interests of the employees, partners, consumers, and general public are also considered, to varying degrees.

- *Family model.* In East Asian and Latin American countries, it is common for corporations to be primarily owned by one family. As a result, these countries tend to have less structured practices of Corporate Governance and place priority on family interests rather than those of all shareholders.

International Corporations

In the past, international corporations have benefited from diminished regulations, the ability to operate in regions with fewer laws, and a perception of unlimited freedom. Additionally, inexpensive labor and lower tax rates have been large factors in drawing company activities away from developed countries and into emerging nations.

These activities have created the image of corporations living a lawless existence in which they are able to manipulate their international standing to avoid penalties, labor codes, and environmental regulations. Although such an existence can assist the company in increasing revenue by limiting expenditures, the actions are frequently unsavory to investors and the general public.

Past years have shown increasing interest in the international activities of corporations, especially those that originate in developed markets and shift all or part of their operations to emerging countries. Public concern centers on environmental and labor practices as well as the effects that international accounting has on share values.

Overall, the message is becoming clear that shareholders and societies do care what happens beyond their borders. As a result, many corporations and organizations are working to improve the image of the international corporation and instill at least a semblance of good Corporate Governance practices. The difficulty that arises in these efforts stems from the unique nature of each marketplace. It is feasible, and common, that an international corporation will exist concurrently in several nations, all of which have their own unique market structures. Frequently, differences in laws and customs will hinder a corporation's ability to apply one uniform set of Corporate Governance policies to all of its subsidiaries.

Organizations such as the Organization of Economic Co-operation and Development (OECD) work toward creating global principles of Corporate Governance that will assist international companies in their governance efforts. These principles are meant to provide a basic foundation on which individual policies can be formed, creating a framework that allows unique circumstances to be accounted for while still maintaining overall cohesion.

The OECD Centre for Co-Operation with Nonmembers

Although its primary focus is with member countries, the Organization of Economic Co-operation and Development also dedicates time and resources to developing relationships with nonmember countries. Those countries that are willing to participate are offered guidance in terms of best practices and assistance in facilitating Corporate Governance discussions with other market members and relevant government bodies.

Global Investors

Domestic corporations often seek to expand their capital base by selling shares to foreign shareholders. When a corporation of one nation lists itself on the market of another nation, it is referred to as a foreign issuer. Two commonly referred to classifications include:

1. *American Depositary Receipts.* An American Depositary Receipt (ADR) is a foreign stock that trades on one of the U.S. exchanges. It is through these stocks that foreign issuers seek to build capital, over and above the levels available within their own domestic markets. In the past, ADRs have been particularly useful for corporations in emerging markets because they create access to a wealth base that would otherwise be unimaginable for these companies. However, growing regulations (such as the Sarbanes-Oxley Act) imposed on foreign issuers are creating some barriers to selling shares on the U.S. markets.

2. *Global Depositary Receipts.* Similar to ADRs, Global Depository Receipts (GDRs) are their counterparts listed on global markets. As U.S. regulations increase for foreign issuers, it may become increasingly possible for them to elect for GDRs instead.

Where once foreign issuers were granted consideration in terms of domestic regulation compliance, now there is a growing trend toward tightening the reins. This is a trend spearheaded by the United States and its mandatory Sarbanes-Oxley Act compliance for all U.S. listed corporations whether foreign issuer or domestic.

Difficulties arise particularly for nations from emerging markets that are either unable to afford the compliance efforts or unable to reconcile the U.S.-based principles with those of their own countries.

Global Corporate Governance Forum

As an initiative between the OECD and the World Bank, the Global Corporate Governance Forum seeks to facilitate discussion of international Corporate Governance frameworks. This forum's general mission also includes efforts to educate the international market on the importance of good Corporate Governance and the benefits that compliance can offer.

Recognizing the unique circumstances of each country and their individual markets, the Global Corporate Governance Forum is supplemented by Regional Policy Dialogue Round Tables.[1] These Round Tables seek to create an understanding of regional demands for Corporate Governance and barriers that stand in the way of policy implementation. The discussions are also aimed at developing strategies and increasing awareness. Finally, one of the principal goals of the

Regional Policy Dialogue Round Tables is to facilitate the local establishment of legally binding and voluntary regulations.

The discussions and emergent results from the Regional Policy Dialogue Round Tables are available through the OECD as Regional White Papers on Corporate Governance downloadable from the OECD web site (www.oecd.com).

IN THE REAL WORLD

International Efforts to Create Good Corporate Governance Policies

Members of the global market recognize that just as Corporate Governance will benefit the individual and the economy in which it is embedded, global Corporate Governance practices will benefit the international economy as a whole.

Many organizations are spearheading the establishment of universal Corporate Governance principles and have been doing so for several decades. Leaders in this objective include:

- *Organization for Economic Co-operation and Development (OECD).* Working with its member countries and those outside of its membership to help establish the groundwork for national Corporate Governance standards

- *International Corporate Governance Network.* Working with investors to increase education efforts and establish Corporate Governance guidelines across international borders

- *Commonwealth Association for Corporate Governance.* Working primarily with African nations to promote the development of good Corporate Governance practices for corporations within the continent

Conclusion

The concept of Corporate Governance and its importance for investors and society as a whole does not stop where a country's borders end. Instead, a corporation's Corporate Governance practices are integral to all its activities, both within the corporation's home nation and internationally.

This chapter discussed the significance of international markets and the impact that the growing global economy has on Corporate Governance practices. Since Corporate Governance is integrally linked to the structure of the corporation and corporate structures vary among countries, it is important to understand these differences and their impact.

Perhaps most significant in this discussion is the implication of internationally run corporations, whose activities pull them across national borders and into widely varying markets. Although once able to exert practices that manipulated their international standing to avoid regulations and laws, these corporations are becoming increasingly aware of the negative image that such behaviors are creating for themselves and their industries.

Investors should to be involved and alert to all material activities of those corporations in which they invest, whether these activities are completed domestically or internationally. As a result, many companies with international subsidiaries and dealings are working to improve their images by implementing good Corporate Governance practices throughout their organizations.

The political, legal, and cultural differences between nations and their corporate structures can present difficulties in achieving international Corporate Governance practices. Those companies that make conscious efforts to do so are not alone, however, and have the support of internationally conscious Corporate Governance organizations such as the OECD.

Summary

- Corporate structure and practices will be influenced by the political, legal, and cultural environment of the corporation's home country.
- International differences demand flexibility in Corporate Governance practices to effectively compensate for varying corporate structures.
- Corporations that exist between international borders are becoming increasingly visible as the global economy spreads.
- International corporations present unique problems for Corporate Governance because they must contend with different structures and regulations within their own company.
- The OECD and World Bank are key players in facilitating the establishment of flexible Corporate Governance frameworks.

Note

1. Stilpon Nestor, "International Efforts to Improve Corporate Governance: Why and How," Organization for Economic Co-Operation and Development, OECD Database, www.oecd.com.

CHAPTER 11

Corporate Governance in Emerging Markets: Asia and Latin America

After reading this chapter, you will be able to:

- Understand the role of Corporate Governance in Asia
- Understand the circumstances created by dictatorships
- Understand the role of Corporate Governance in Latin America

In Chapter 10 we discussed the significance of the international market and its role in shaping the face of Corporate Governance policies. Global economics is a complex and involved concept that consists of several interrelated issues. A thorough discussion of global economics and international policies is beyond the scope of this book.

Instead, this chapter presents the issues of Corporate Governance as they relate to the emerging economies of Asia and Latin America. It is important to remember that each of these economies holds within it several distinct markets and unique corporate structures. However, this general overview will provide sufficient context for gaining an expanded perspective on global Corporate Governance.

Asia

A common theme in the profiles of many Asian corporations is that they are family owned. In fact, family-owned firms represent anywhere from one-half to two-thirds of the publicly traded corporations of any given Asian country.[1]

A second corporate feature of Asian companies is the pyramid structure, where one parent company operates partnerships and ownerships of several subsidiaries. The culminating effect of family ownerships and complex webs of subsidiaries is a system in which transparency is difficult to foster and nonfamily investors are not afforded the same privileges as the family.[2]

The ubiquitous nature of family relationships within and between corporations in Asian countries also fosters informal rather than regulated stakeholder relationships. This can create uncertainties for foreign investors who prefer a transparent system by which they can monitor their investment.

Overall, the traditional corporate structure of Asian companies is not consistent with the U.S. ideal of upholding shareholder rights. Entrenched family priorities and information relationships can create wariness and hesitation in foreign investors. Recognizing this, members of Asian public markets are working to establish greater transparency and stronger formal regulations.[3]

Attempts are being made to establish these good Corporate Governance practices across Asian nations:

- *Improved reporting requirements.* An overall movement toward improved reporting requirements has been initiated in many countries, although the actual regulations vary between countries and regions. The reports may be audited or unaudited, depending on local regulations. They may also be released annually, biannually, or quarterly.

- *Increased fairness in voting practices.* It is now generally accepted that shareholder voting rights are based on the "one share, one vote" principle.

- *Increased involvement in director election.* Although not all regions allow shareholders to nominate potential directors, they do provide the right for shareholders to participate in director elections.[4]

IN THE REAL WORLD

The Red Corporations

The Shanghai Stock Exchange (SHSE) was established in 1990 and holds the distinction of being the first communist stock exchange; the Shenzhen Stock Exchange (SZSE) was the second.

The unique circumstances of the Chinese market and its implications for Corporate Governance and other corporate matters are discussed in Jian Chen's *Corporate Governance in China*.[a] According to Chen, a primary motivation for the establishment of publicly traded Chinese corporations is a desire to generate capital to facilitate further expansion of the Chinese economy.

Chen further explains that the political circumstances of the past and present have implications regarding the establishment of good Corporate Governance practices.

Unique circumstances of the Chinese market include:

- Its involvement in moving from concepts of "soft" to "hard" debt as the government switches from owner to shareholder
- State control of the sale of shares of many Chinese corporations
- Prohibition of seasonal equity offerings

[a] Jian Chen, *Corporate Governance in China* (New York, RoutledgeCourzon, 2004).

Latin America

As the economies of Latin American countries become increasingly privatized, the importance of good Corporate Governance practices is an emerging concern. Generally speaking, the bulk of capital activity in these regions has fallen on the public sector and small companies within the private sector.[5]

Encouraging private sector growth and the establishment of a greater corporate population requires heightened investment in the marketplace, which can be facilitated by increasing market security and trust through good Corporate Governance practices. Of great importance in Latin America, as in many other markets, is the encouragement of foreign investment.

Attracting foreign investment presents complications of its own, however, as countries are increasingly regulating those companies to which they offer depository receipts. For example, foreign issuers seeking to list on U.S. markets through American Depositary Receipts (ADRs) are now required to comply with U.S. regulations, such as the Sarbanes-Oxley Act.

Requirements such as these create problems for corporations in Latin America and other regions as they struggle to meet foreign regulations with already limited capital. The solution has been to work toward establishing Corporate Governance frameworks on which corporations will be built to ensure general compliance with international regulations and promote confidence in the local markets.

A large part of Latin American Corporate Governance efforts have been toward creating greater activity in terms of ADRs and Global Depository Receipts (GDRs). To encourage foreign investment in the corporations of Latin American countries, it is important that foreign investors feel secure that their rights will be respected. This means that foreign shareholders require assurance that they will have a facilitated right to vote, ability to bring forth proposals, and ability to enjoy all of the same rights offered to domestic owners.

Further efforts that have been made toward good Corporate Governance in Latin American countries include:

- *Instituto Argentino para el Gobierno de las Organiaciones (IAGO)*. This organization, established in 2002 in Argentina, was a joint effort of FUNDECE and IDEA, two private sector organizations intent on improving Corporate Governance education, particularly for members of corporate boards of directors.

- *Novo Mercado*. The top tier of the three levels on the Sao Paulo Stock Exchange (BOVESPA). This hierarchy within the market creates distinct levels of required Corporate Governance compliance efforts. In order to list at the highest level, corporations must offer accurate and complete disclosure of financial information and strongly uphold investor rights, among other requirements.

TIPS AND TECHNIQUES

Compliance with International Financial Reporting Standards

In order to provide foreign shareholders with information regarding their investments, those corporations traded on foreign markets should offer their financial information in compliance with the International Financial Reporting Standards (IFRS).

Although these standards are nonbinding, voluntary compliance with them will assure investors that they are receiving accurate and complete information. These standards are particularly significant in those countries where national guidelines have not been established.

It is still important, however, that corporations already complying with national reporting standards offer international investors the added security of incorporating the IFRS recommendations into their practices.

Conclusion

Corporations in emerging markets carry more than just their own success on their shoulders. Should they thrive, these corporations will foster the triumph of the market itself and buoy the country's economic situation. However, should enough corporations in an emerging market fail, they could cause its economy to collapse.

It is for this reason that good Corporate Governance policies are so important in emerging markets. A strong reputation of good Corporate Governance will foster trust and encourage international investors to invest in the market. Additionally, good Corporate Governance practices will increase the likelihood of corporate success by securing the companies against fraud and scandal.

Countries in Asia and Latin America are fast creating a strong presence on the international market. In order for their companies to compete effectively with more established corporations, they must shorten their learning curves and embrace good Corporate Governance sooner rather than later.

Summary

- Unlike the U.S. model, the Asian corporate structure is largely dominated by family-controlled corporations.

- Recommendations to improve Corporate Governance policies in emerging Asian markets include an increased focus on regulated reporting requirements, fair voting practices, and representative director elections.

- The emerging markets of Latin America place a great focus on securing foreign investment.

Notes

1. Organization for Economic Co-operation and Development, "White Paper on Corporate Governance in Asia," 2003, www.OECD.org.

2. Jian Chen, *Corporate Governance in China* (New York: Routledge Courzon, 2004).

3. OECD, "White Paper on Corporate Governance in Asia."

4. OECD, "White Paper on Corporate Governance in Asia."

5. Organization for Economic Co-operation and Development, "White Paper on Corporate Governance in Latin America," 2003, www.OECD.org.

CHAPTER 12

Not-for-Profit Organizations

After reading this chapter, you will be able to

- Understand what a nonprofit or not-for-profit corporation is
- Understand the differences between for-profit and not-for-profit corporations
- Understand the value of good Corporate Governance practices for not-for-profit organizations
- Understand the systems through which not-for-profit corporations can work to enhance their Corporate Governance practices

During the discussion of Corporate Governance in publicly traded corporations, the concept of market image was discussed in terms of good Corporate Governance promoting the investors' trust in the entire market. This same principle can apply to a discussion of not-for-profit corporations.

When scandal and fraud occur in any area of the economy, the public becomes outraged, but when it happens in a charitable organization, the consequences are exponentially dire. For many people, it is unimaginable that anyone would steal from an organization that has been established in the spirit of charity. Even more upsetting are situations in which the organizations themselves are misusing, mishandling, or exploiting donated resources rather than allocating them to the intended purpose.

Unfortunately, what happens in one instance can taint the public's perception of an entire sector. As such, it is important for all not-for-profit organizations to enhance their efforts toward good Corporate Governance practices as a way to promote the public's general level of trust.

This chapter discusses the not-for-profit corporation and how it differs from a for-profit corporation. It elaborates on the concept of good Corporate Governance and public trust, while elucidating the methods in which not-for-profit corporations can establish strong practices of Corporate Governance to the benefit of themselves, those they serve, and the nonprofit sector as a whole.

Nonprofit and For-Profit Corporations

Intuitively when we think of corporations, we think of those with stocks that are traded on public markets, and are owned by shareholders. Although this is one form of corporation, there is another: the not-for-profit corporation.

EXHIBIT 12.1

For-Profit and Not-for-Profit Corporations

For-Profit Corporation	Not-for-Profit Corporation
Offers shares on the public markets	Is prohibited from selling shares
Primary responsibility is to shareholders	Responsibility is to a variety of stakeholders
Governed by a charter	
Operates with an elected board of directors	

Although both are corporations, for-profit and not-for-profit corporations differs in several ways.

Legally speaking, corporations can be established for a wide variety of purposes, one of which is to transfer ownership from private hands to those of shareholders. In situations where shareholders own stock in a corporation, they are entitled to the profits in the form of dividends during the life of the corporation and asset divisions after its dissolution.

A not-for-profit, or nonprofit, corporation, however, does not sell shares to investors and is not traded on the public markets. Often these nonprofit corporations are established as part of the process of opening fundraising channels available only to charitable corporations. (See Exhibit 12.1 for a comparison of for-profit and not-for-profit corporations.)

TIPS AND TECHNIQUES

Identifying the Form of a Not-for-Profit Organization

Just as for-profit businesses can take many legal forms, so can not-for-profit organizations. Incorporating is one of several options for establishing a charitable organization. The selection of incorporation over other options will depend on the organization's unique circumstances. Some typical types of nonprofits are:

- *Foundations.* Foundations are bodies that are established to collect and manage donations. These organizations are not the final destination for the donations, but are instead charged with the distribution of resources to the appropriate charities.

- *Trusts.* Trusts are established to ensure that a charitable act is carried out as part of an estate.

- *Associations.* Associations are collectives of members that are, in theory, run by those members. However, it is more likely that employees will join an association as a condition of employment rather than that the association will hire solely from within its membership body.

Stakeholders, Not Shareholders

Not-for-profit corporations are not traded on markets and are prohibited from paying dividends. Although they do not have shareholders, not-for-profit corporations and their boards do have obligations to stakeholders.

In terms of the not-for-profit corporate structure, the stakeholders are the same as those in for-profit organizations, with the exclusion of the shareholder. These stakeholders include employees, volunteers, nonshareholder investors, and others who offer financial and nonfinancial support.

It is for these parties that the not-for-profit corporation establishes practices of good Corporate Governance, although the fiduciary duties applied to boards with shareholders do not exist here. Additionally, these organizations also establish practices for good Corporate Governance to sustain themselves for the benefit of the demographic they were established to serve.

IN THE REAL WORLD

Not–for–Profit Corporation's Stakeholders

Unlike their for-profit counterparts, the not-for-profit corporation is not accountable to shareholders. Instead, its responsibility lies in meeting the needs of other stakeholders.

As discussed, the term "stakeholder" can be applied to anyone that has a vested interest in the corporation. For-profit corporations are primarily concerned with the interest of one type of stakeholder, the shareholder. Not-for-profits are responsible to many types of stakeholders, including:

- *Founder.* The founder of a not-for-profit corporation may be active in the running of the organization or may not have any involvement at all. An active founder will have an emotional stake in the organization, and as the creator will likely feel a strong desire for its success. Even an absent founder's interests are often still present within the organization in terms of a mission statement or similar document.

- *Clients.* Not-for-profit corporations have a primary concern with meeting the needs of those they have been established to aid. Should the organization cease to meet this need, its existence would no longer be worthwhile, and the organization would begin to collapse.

- *Employees and volunteers.* Given the relatively low budgets of many not-for-profit organizations, sustaining a force of volunteers is integral to their operation. In order to retain this "free labor," the not-for-profit must be able to meet the volunteers' needs successfully and encourage them to continue their services pro bono.

  Even many employees accept a lower pay rate in order to work for a cause in which they believe. That not-for-profits rely on labor at

Underlying Principles

The motivations of establishing good Corporate Governance practices within not-for-profit corporations are different from those of their for-profit counterparts. Not-for-profits are not striving to improve trust and relationships with stockholders, but are instead working to improve trust and relationships with philanthropic investors.

As a result of these differences, the goals of Corporate Governance will vary between the two classes of corporation, but the underlying principles remain the same. Most not-for-profits' major objectives and principles include:

- *Protecting the corporation's financial health.* The board of directors of a publicly traded corporation is responsible for protecting shareholder investments by sustaining the corporation's financial health. Not-for-profit corporations have the same objective:

to protect their own longevity by establishing practices that are fiscally responsible.

TIPS AND TECHNIQUES

Fiscally Responsible Practices for Not-for-Profit Corporations

Not-for-profit corporations and their management must work toward sustaining the organization through fiscally responsible decisions and practices. Some integral Corporate Governance policies that facilitate this goal include:

- *Establishing sound accounting practices* that include adequate controls to protect the integrity and accuracy of financial records.

- *Hiring independent auditors* who are reliable and reputable.

- *Adopting a responsible budget* that considers long-term goals as well as prudent ideals.

- *Establishing a regular schedule for budget reviews* to ensure that the framework is accurate, up-to-date, and reflective of the organization's current situation and goals.

- *Protecting integral network relationships.* A for-profit corporation exists within an extended web of companies and individuals, both domestic and international, which support its success through services, investments, and partnerships. The creation of these relationships, although beneficial, can be a costly process. It is therefore important that the health of these relationships is closely monitored and maintained. Similarly, not-for-profit corporations often rely heavily on volunteers and other community member relationships. Not only do network members provide financial support, they also offer services and other valuable resources.

Developing and Sustaining Relationships for Not-for-Profit Corporations

Not-for-profit corporations rely on strong community ties for donated and purchased resources. Most not-for-profit organizations run a great deal of their activities through volunteer efforts and financial donations. Gaining access to these resources, as well as maintaining the support, is integral to sustaining the organization's efforts.

Additionally, as with all other organizations, not-for-profit corporations require skilled support from several industries, including accounting services, maintenance, consultants, and legal assistance. It is in the organization's best fiscal interest to secure not only a good price, but also high quality. In many cases, service providers are willing to offer discounts or volunteer their services for charity. Establishing and maintaining such relationships should be a high priority of every not-for-profit organization.

Establishing and sustaining relationships requires a strong commitment toward effective communication both with the community as a whole and with individual supporters. Efforts that will facilitate this goal include:

- Bulletins that communicate the organization's updates and activities
- Marketing strategies
- Media relations
- Open policies between board members and volunteers
- Systems and schedules for showing appreciation

Corporate Governance for Small Not-for-Profit Organizations

Generally speaking, guidelines and recommendations that address Corporate Governance for not-for-profit corporations are geared toward large organizations with strong infrastructures and large resource pools in terms of both finances and personnel.

Establishing a strong set of Corporate Governance policies can be difficult for small not-for-profit organizations that have limited resources in terms of time, money, and personnel. Instead of curtailing their efforts, however, these small organizations can find ways to establish good Corporate Governance without breaking the bank. For example:

- *Start right away.* Not-for-profit corporations that embed good Corporate Governance policies in their first charter draft will have an easier time continuing with their efforts.

- *Play up the strengths.* Small not-for-profits do have advantages in Corporate Governance that larger organizations do not have. The smaller the group, the greater the control of the board and executive. Smaller groups also facilitate more transparency within the system. Finally, small not-for-profits can have a higher degree of communication between stakeholders and the board.

Small not-for-profit corporations can improve their Corporate Governance efforts by adapting these recommendations to suit the scale of their operations:

- Identify and eliminate all/most conflicts of interest among board members, executive members, and key personnel.

- Separate the functions and positions of the board and the executive, while working hard to establish as independent a board as possible.

Tips and Techniques (continued)

- Establish a comprehensive code of ethics, create a training schedule for all key organization members, and publish it for stakeholders to view.

- Establish processes that protect the confidentiality and integrity of whistle-blowers within the organization. This may include assigning an independent board member to the position of compliance officer.

- Establish secure accounting principles that account for full disclosure to relevant parties and regulated document destruction.

Improved Security of Accounting Practices

A large component of improving Corporate Governance policies in for-profit corporations is the establishment of secure accounting practices to protect the funds of investors and prevent the corporation from falling to bankruptcy due to scandal. Improved security of accounting practices is equally important in not-for-profit corporations that are also charged with protecting the funds of others. In this case, the money belongs in part to those who have donated it and in part to those whom the services are meant to help.

One strategy that many not-for-profit organizations have found viable is voluntary compliance with the Sarbanes-Oxley (SOX) Act. Such a move provides the organizations with guidance in terms of how to implement the changes to secure their financial records and also boosts their public image as trustworthy organizations.

Compelled into Voluntary Sarbanes–Oxley Compliance

The Sarbanes-Oxley Act requires that publicly traded corporations comply with its regulations as a safeguard to protect investors from misleading financial information. Although not legally compelled to do so, many not-for-profit organizations and corporations are establishing systems for voluntary SOX compliance. The motivations for doing so range from increased security within the organization to improved public image as a trustworthy organization.

There are also circumstances in which not-for-profit organizations may be compelled to comply with SOX, although not by the Public Company Accounting Oversight Board. Other institutions that enter into agreements with a not-for-profit organization may demand that the organization be deemed SOX compliant as assurance that their financial donation will be well looked after.

In situations such as these, compliance is still considered voluntary in the sense that it is not legally mandated, and there is no legal retribution for noncompliance.

Benefits of Good Corporate Governance for Not-for-Profit Corporations

Not-for-profit corporations that establish strong Corporate Governance practices will enjoy many benefits, not only in terms of their public image, but in the efficacy with which their organizations are run. It is easy to forget, as we discuss Corporate Governance, that it is not simply a hoop through which corporations jump to appease investors; it is a system of best practices that improve the functioning of the corporations themselves.

In terms of improved operations, not-for-profit corporations that evaluate their current Corporate Governance practices and work to enhance them will benefit from:

- *Fraud protection.* It is an unfortunate reality that even not-for-profit corporations are not immune to the threat of fraud and other criminal activities, from external as well as internal culprits. By enhancing the systems and policies that promote good Corporate Governance, these organizations can increase their protection against falling victim to corruption. In return, they will be able to sustain their ethical image and further promote donations to their cause.

- *Greater internal organization.* Good Corporate Governance practices require a strong internal framework between the roles of the board of directors and those of the executive. Establishing clear job descriptions and outlining the functions of board members in contrast to those of executive members is a task too often neglected. Yet when these two groups clearly understand their obligations and boundaries, the organization will enjoy a heightened level of productivity and a limited amount of conflict.

- *Improved relationships with stakeholders.* A not-for-profit corporation that seeks to strengthen its Corporate Governance policies will likely include efforts toward improving stakeholder communications as part of its strategy. Offering stakeholders greater access to a more transparent organization helps assure them that they are putting their donations in the right place and that their funds are not being abused. The increased level of communication also aids in the fostering of closer relationships between the stakeholders and board, which can lead to its own benefits of increased support later on.

Ideal Not-for-Profit Corporate Governance Profile

A not-for-profit corporation can facilitate its own success by taking an inventory of its strengths and weaknesses and building its Corporate Governance policies to improve all areas of operation. A thorough consideration of the corporate structure will include evaluations in many areas including:

- *Relationships.* As in all corporations, the communication and working relationships that exist among board members, among executive members, and between the two groups are vital to sustaining a healthy organization. Although these relationships do not have to be built on kinship, they must have a semblance of amicability and a strong foundation of integrity and respect.

  Any breakdown of the internal communication or the purposeful establishment of barriers will create problems for the effective running of the association. When relationship problems are identified within the corporation, the board should take the initiative in establishing policies to rectify the situation before it further hinders productivity.

  A large factor in the maintenance of effective relationships is the creation of clear role descriptions and boundaries. When all members of the organization understand their role and the expectations associated with it, there will be less chance of members overstepping their stations or failing to meet their obligations.

Another important part of the solution is establishing clear channels for conflict resolution. These can include the establishment of a subcommittee for the purpose of identifying and mitigating problems as well as provisions for arbitration in more serious cases.

- *Respect of stakeholder interests.* As discussed earlier in this chapter, not-for-profit corporations have responsibilities to their stakeholders, even though this group does not include shareholders. A board that exhibits a high ethical standard and strong leadership is integral to sustaining stakeholder trust. Also important is cohesion among the stakeholders and their views of the organization's best interest.

  Unlike for-profit corporations, the board of a not-for-profit corporation does not have a fiduciary duty to the stakeholders. Instead, the duty of board members extends only to fostering confidence and a willingness to further contribute to the organization's success. It is for this reason that unified values and ideals are beneficial. The creation of such solidarity can be achieved through education and communication on the part of the board.

- *Strong internal policies and practices.* Establishing a framework in which all members adhere to internal policies and practices will facilitate smooth functioning of the organization. These policies include effective training strategies, a regular schedule for training updates, a comprehensive code of ethics, standards for structured meetings, and clear expectations with fair reprimands for violating policies.

Conclusion

In principle, the existence of not-for-profit organizations is based on the same concept as the for-profit publicly traded corporation: voluntary investment on the part of the public. Although not legally compelled to establish good Corporate Governance practices such as SOX, not-for-profit corporations have strong motivations for doing so.

In an effort to gain and sustain the trust of philanthropic individuals and groups, many not-for-profit corporations are making concerted efforts toward improving their transparency, securing the accuracy of their financial records, and strengthening the governing capabilities of their boards.

Summary

- Not-for-profit corporations are chartered entities that are not able to sell stock or pay dividends.

- Not-for-profit corporations do not have shareholders as members of their stakeholder group but do have others with vested interests in the organization, such as employees, volunteers, donors, and the sectors they have been established to serve.

- Good Corporate Governance practices for not-for-profit corporations will work to protect their financial health and secure their relationship with stakeholders and the general public.

- Many not-for-profit corporations are voluntarily complying with financial reporting and accounting regulations such as the Sarbanes-Oxley Act.

Afterword

anjay and I have worked together, shared ideas, and even collaborated on books. So when I was invited to write an afterword for this book, it was an easy decision to say yes.

My professional passion is Corporate Governance and compliance. Of course, a large portion of the articles and books I write deal with the action aspects of the topic: how to comply with laws and regulations, explaining to corporations that good Corporate Governance is good for profit, and so on. Yet my true goal, and I see it in this book, is to change the mentality and mind-set so that good Corporate Governance becomes second nature and intrinsic in business practices.

We will have a stronger corporate culture once this is achieved.

The first step on the journey to changing the way the world views business is to change the internal, emotive standards of people. People run businesses. I, Sanjay, and others like us can spend all day explaining to boards why good Corporate Governance is good for business, but we would be more readily heard if societal norms supported our assertions.

Once society supports and demands, as it is starting to, a standard of corporate behavior that holds good Corporate Governance as the pinnacle of business, then we can truly start making some headway.

Afterword

This book reaches several layers in the corporate world, from the CEO to the consumer. Now that you have read it, you can start not only applying the principles of good Corporate Governance but also working to change your own internal standards to which you hold corporate culture.

If you are an executive or director, then this book has provided you with information on your legal and ethical duties toward the Corporate Governance practices of your corporation. Will you take this information and comply with the minimum standards, or will you put this information toward creating a market advantage for your company?

Your investors and consumers are becoming a highly educated and business-aware demographic. They are growing to understand what they require to receive the greatest benefits, and they will look to your company to provide them. This is your opportunity to excel and surpass your competition.

If you are a company employee, I applaud you for having read this book and for taking the initiative to learn about Corporate Governance. Now you understand that Corporate Governance is not a topic reserved solely for the boardroom but one that impacts all company members.

When we think about the corporations that fell to scandal in the late 1990s, we can see waves of unemployed company members now forced to start over. You have taken a step toward protecting yourself from a similar fate. I encourage you to continue learning and asking questions. Read more books on the topic and educate yourself further so that when your executives and board members make a decision, you will be in a position to critically evaluate it.

If you are an investor, then this book has provided you with information about rights that many investors do not understand. Now you know that investor relations should be held to a high standard, rather than relegated to the sidelines of business activity.

I read this book as a Corporate Governance professional, an investor, and a member of the economy in which corporations reign. We are all part of that economy, and when corporations go astray it is we who feel the fall. Take the motivation you feel after reading this book and seek out more information so that, as a global community, we can create good Corporate Governance and business practices of which we can be proud.

Anthony Tarantino, Ph.D., Six Sigma Blackbelt

Senior Advisor, IBM, Governance, Risk, and Compliance Center of Excellence

Author of *The Manager's Guide to Compliance* (John Wiley & Sons, 2006)

and *Compliance Handbook: Technology, Finance, Environmental, and International Guidance and Best Practices* (John Wiley & Sons, 2007)

Guide to the *Combined Code on Corporate Governance* and its Similarities to Corporate Governance in the American Model

The *Combined Code on Corporate Governance* (2003) is a U.K. code that came into effect in late 2003. One of the most important factors of this code is that it operates on the principle of "if not, why not?" This principle is a statement of understanding that the code will be applied in all situations, except those where departure can be reasonably explained.

Code Of Best Practice

Section 1 Companies

A. Directors

A.1 The Board

This section of the code dictates the importance of establishing a board and lays out members' general obligations and duties, which include:

- Regular meetings of all board members
- Regular meetings between the chairperson and the non-executive directors
- Publishing of an annual report
- The taking of meeting minutes
- Obtaining insurance for board members

Indemnities, although an attractive addition to compensation plans, are not a necessary component in the U.S. corporate structure. In fact, there is some argument that their inclusion could reduce the effectiveness of the fiduciary duties of board members.

A.2 The Chairman and Chief Executive

This section of the code mandates that the powers of chairperson and chief executive be held by two individuals. It further stipulates that the chairperson should meet the criteria of independence outlined in A.3.

A.3 Board Balance and Independence

This section states that the board should be balanced between executive and nonexecutive members to facilitate board independence. Members would be considered independent if they:

- Have been a company employee in the past five years
- Have conducted material business with the company within the last five years
- Receive compensation from the company outside of board fees
- Represent a material shareholder
- Have exceeded nine years of service on the board

This section further states that at least half of the board should meet the criteria of independence and that board members should appoint a senior independent director.

A.4 Appointments to the Board

This section outlines the procedures for appointing new directors to the board, which include:

- Establishment of a nomination committee
- Evaluation of the current board by the nomination committee
- Preparation of a job outline for the positions that will be filled, particularly when it is a chairperson position that is becoming vacant

Section A.4 further states that the board should not appoint a full-time director who has directorship on other FTSE (*Financial Times* stock exchange) 100 companies of the London Stock Exchange.

Although there is concern that busy board members will be unable to fulfill their duty effectively, directors sitting on multiple boards are not uncommon in the U.S. corporate structure.

A.5 Information and Professional Development

This section states that board members should receive the information and training that they require to fulfill their tasks effectively.

In the U.S. corporate model, the responsibility for gathering adequate information lies with the individual directors. Not being presented with the information is not sufficient justification for a fiduciary duty violation.

A.6 Performance Evaluation

This section states that the board should evaluate itself and its committees once a year. The results from the evaluation should be noted in the annual report.

A.7 Reelection

This section calls for planned turnovers within the board with a maximum term of three years. At the end of their term, directors must be reelected by shareholders at the annual meeting.

B. Remuneration

B.1 Level and Makeup of Remuneration

While this section recognizes that the compensation must be sufficient to attract quality directors, it does charge the board to pay only as much as necessary. It also states that award-based compensation should comprise the bulk of the compensation package.

This section states that nonexecutive directors should not be granted share options.

There is argument in the U.S. model that supports granting stock options to all directors in an effort to align their interests with those of the shareholders.

B.2 Procedure

This section recommends that corporations establish policies for the development of compensation packages. One key policy is that board members are not put in a conflict of interest and allowed to determine their own compensation. The provisions of this section outline the establishment of a compensation committee.

C. Accountability and Audit

C.1 Financial Reporting

This section states that the financial records should be accurate and representative. It further recommends that the annual report provide this information.

C.2 Internal Control

This section requires that the board protect shareholder investment and company assets through control systems.

In the U.S. corporate model, the responsibility for establishing such controls lies with the chief executive and chief financial officers, according to the Sarbanes-Oxley Act.

C.3 Audit Committee and Auditors

In establishing the financial reporting controls, the board should ensure that the policies are formally described and the processes are transparent. Further provisions of this section include:

- The establishment of an audit committee that has a minimum of three members, one of whom has adequate financial experience.
- The audit committee will monitor the integrity of the financial reports and their controls.
- The audit committee will make recommendations.
- The external auditor's involvement in nonaudit ways should be limited and carefully monitored.

The provisions of this section are similar to those mandated by the Sarbanes-Oxley Act.

Directory of Select Corporate Governance Organizations Around the World

Asian Corporate Governance Association. Founded in 1999, the Asian Corporate Governance Association (ACGA) is an independent, nonprofit organization that seeks to promote Corporate Governance in emerging Asian economies. This organization works to facilitate Corporate Governance development through research, advocacy, and education. Further information can be found through its Web site: www.acga-asia.org.

Commonwealth Association for Corporate Governance Inc. Founded in 1998, the Commonwealth Association for Corporate Governance (CACG) is an association for the promotion of international standards of Corporate Governance throughout the commonwealth. Further information can be found through its Web site: www.cacg-inc.com.

Institute on Governance. Established in 1990 out of Canada, the Institute on Governance (IOG) is a nonprofit organization that seeks to promote Corporate Governance efforts. This organization works to facilitate the practical implementation of Corporate Governance principles in public corporations and those organizations seeking voluntary inclusion. Further information can be found through its Web site: www.iog.ca.

Organization for Economic Co-operation and Development. Working with 30 member countries and 70 nonmember countries, the Organization of Economic Co-operation and Development (OECD) strives to foster good governance in public service and corporate activity. This organization produces documents, decisions, and recommendations, such as the *OECD Principles of Corporate Governance.* Further information can be found through its Web site: www.oecd.org.

Society of Corporate Secretaries and Governance Professionals. Founded in 1946, the society was originally called the American Society of Corporate Secretaries. This society is involved in education, advocacy, and the communication of information. Further information can be found through its Web site: www.governanceprofessionals.org.

Glossary

Agency loss The amount of money that a principal loses in deferring operations to an agent. In terms of corporate structure, agency loss refers to the difference between the amount that shareholders would make if they ran operations versus assigning the task to corporate management.

Agency theory A theory regarding the relationship between principals and agents. In Corporate Governance terms, the principals are the shareholders and the agents are the managers.

American Depositary Receipts (ADRs) Shares of foreign companies that are sold on the U.S. markets through an intermediary, usually a bank.

Association A collective of members that is, in theory, run by those members.

Audit committee Subdivision of the board of directors that monitors the corporation's compliance with Securities and Exchange Commission and Public Company Accounting Oversight Board regulations.

Auditor An independent assessor who conducts a systematic check or assessment. In the case of Corporate Governance, it is an assessment of internal controls of publicly traded companies.

Berle, Adolf Coauthor of *The Modern Corporation and Private Property,* his theories detail the differences between corporate management and shareholder owners.

Board of directors The governing body of a corporation responsible for providing direction and guidance for the working of the organization.

Business judgment rule Establishes the legal obligations of the board of directors, while limiting its liability to those circumstances when best, reasonable judgment was not employed.

Cadbury Report Also known as the Cadbury Commission's *Financial Aspects of Corporate Governance,* this report offers guidelines for corporations within the United Kingdom and around the world.

Capital structure The system that a corporation has in place to finance itself. This includes a combination of equity sales and options, bonds, and loans.

Carver model A model of governance in which the board of directors appoints an executive to run the organization. Although similar to the traditional model of governance, the Carver model does not include the establishment of board subcommittees.

C corporation A corporation that experiences double taxation; both the corporation's revenues and shareholder dividends are taxed.

Chairperson The head of the board of directors. General duties include presiding over board meetings.

Chief executive officer (CEO) The board-appointed leader of a corporation's executive. The CEO's primary role is to run the company in a successful manner and secure the value of the shareholders' stock.

Code of ethics A set of rules according to which people in a particular profession are expected to model their behaviors and decisions.

Collective model A model of governance in which all company members are involved in decisions and service delivery.

Committee of Sponsoring Organizations (COSO) An internal control framework used in achieving Sarbanes-Oxley compliance.

Commonwealth Association for Corporate Governance An organization that works with African corporations, and those corporations operating on the continent, to create good Corporate Governance practices.

Compensation committee Subdivision of the board of directors that is responsible for establishing and monitoring the corporation's remuneration packages and policies.

Control Objectives for Informational and Related Technology (COBIT) The most popular internal information technology control framework for companies seeking Sarbanes-Oxley compliance.

Corporate Governance committee Subdivision of the board of directors that is responsible for establishing and monitoring efforts to meet the principles of Corporate Governance.

Corporate raiders Those who acquire a controlling interest in a company without the necessary intent of completing a takeover.

Customer relationship management (CRM) A software strategy that is adopted by companies that would like to improve efficiency and revenue by fostering customer loyalty.

Duty of care A fiduciary duty of company directors requiring that they make all reasonable efforts to ensure that their decisions benefit the company.

Duty of loyalty A fiduciary duty of company directors requiring that they act on behalf of the company's interests rather than their own.

Duty of supervision As a component of the duty of care, the duty of supervision relates to the board members' duties of oversight of the executive.

Enterprise Resource Planning (ERP) software A platform to integrate all of a company's departments and functions into one dynamic system.

Entrenchment A situation in which a member of the board or executive is impeding the success of the corporation but cannot be removed readily.

Ethics The general concept of establishing a set of principles that guide actions through values and morals.

Executive directors Board members who function full-time within the management of the company.

Foreign issuer International companies that are traded on the U.S. markets.

Foundation A body that is established to collect and manage donations. A foundation is not the final destination for the donations, but instead is charged with the distribution of resources to the appropriate charities.

Generally accepted accounting principles (GAAP) Procedures and standards to guide companies as they assemble their financial statements. The prime objective of these standards is to provide a common reporting system so that investors have a way to compare companies.

Global Corporate Governance Forum   An open nonprofit forum for discussing Corporate Governance around the world.

Global Depository Receipts (GDRs)   Similar to American Depository Receipts (ADRs), GDRs are their counterparts listed on global markets.

Health Insurance Portability and Accountability Act (HIPAA)   A U.S. act that requires companies to create systems to protect the privacy and security of their employees' health insurance–related documents.

Hostile takeover   A takeover in which an aggressor company acquires enough shares to control the victim company. In time, the aggressor company will push out the former board members and executive, taking their place.

Independent directors   Also known as nonexecutive directors, these are board members who are not otherwise employed by the company.

Instituto Argentino para el Gobierno de las Organiaciones (IAGO)   An Argentinian organization established in 2002 for the purpose of corporate board member education in the concepts of good Corporate Governance.

Interlocks (aka interlocking directorates)   Situations in which the boards of two distinct corporations share one or more members, thus creating a conflict of interest.

International Corporate Governance Network   An organization that works with investors to further their interests and facilitate the establishment of international Corporate Governance practices.

International Financial Reporting Standards (IFRS) A set of nonbinding regulations designed to create an international benchmark for corporate accounting and information disclosure.

Limited liability corporation (LLC) Similar to S corporations, this business form is one in which the revenues of the corporation itself are taxed in addition to those of the shareholders.

Limited liability partnership (LLP) A business form in which all partners enjoy the benefits of limited liability. See also *limited partners*; *partnership.*

Limited partners Members of a business that is built on the partnership form. Limited partners are generally not involved in the operations of the business to a full extent and are often subject to liability that extends only to their investment, not to their personal assets. See also *limited liability partnership.*

Management model A model of governance in which the board governs and runs the corporation without appointing a distinct executive body. Although similar to the operational model, this model includes the hiring of paid staff.

Means, Gardiner Coauthor of *The Modern Corporation and Private Property,* his theories detail the differentiation between corporate management and shareholder owners.

National Institute of Standards and Technology (NIST) A nonregulatory federal agency that was established within the U.S. Commerce Department's Technology Administration in 1901.

Nominating committee Subdivision of the board of directors that establishes board membership criteria and nominates directors for election or reelection.

Not-for-profit corporation   A chartered organization that does not sell shares and is prohibited from paying dividends. Not-for-profit corporations maintain a similar structure to their for-profit counterparts, usually including a board and executive.

Novo Mercado   The top tier of the Sao Paulo Stock Exchange in terms of Corporate Governance requirements for listing.

Operational model   A model of governance in which the board governs and runs the corporation without appointing a distinct executive body. Although similar to the management model, this model does not include the hiring of paid staff; instead the organization runs with volunteers.

Organization for Economic Co-operation and Development (OECD)   An organization that contains 30 member countries and offers resources and guidance to aid governments in establishing Corporate Governance policies. One of its best-known documents is *OECD Principles of Corporate Governance*.

Partnership   A business form in which one or more of the company's owners are also involved in the operations of the business. This form of business is similar to a proprietorship, except that in a proprietorship, all business owners are involved in operations. See also *limited partners*; *limited liability partnership*.

Poison pill   A strategy to prevent a hostile takeover by flooding the market with shares in order to defeat the aggressor's attempt to acquire a majority.

Proprietorship   A business form in which the owner or owners are also in charge of the company's operations. This is similar to a partnership, except that in partnerships, all partners need not be involved in the operational side of the business.

Public Company Accounting Oversight Board (PCAOB) An organization created by the Sarbanes-Oxley Act to oversee the auditors of public companies and their activities.

Regulation 14a-8 The section of the 1934 U.S. Securities Exchange Act that governs the process by which shareholders are able to submit proposals.

Restricted stock Part of a director's or executive's compensation package, restricted stock is owned by the individual but carries sale-regulating provisions.

Sarbanes-Oxley (SOX) Act U.S. legislation that creates guidelines for corporate accounting and financial reporting procedures.

SAS 70 A document that certifies that the service organization has received an in-depth audit of its relevant internal controls.

S corporation A corporation in which revenue passes directly into shareholder dividends without first being taxed at the corporation level.

Shanghai Stock Exchange (SHSE) Established in 1990, the first stock exchange to be created within the structure of a communist country.

Shareholder An entity (individual or corporation) that legally owns one or more shares of stock in a joint stock company. A company's shareholders collectively own that company.

Shareholder proposal A recommendation made by an owner of corporation stock that the board of directors take a specified action.

Stakeholder   One who has a vested interest in the success of the company. Although this includes shareholders, it is not limited to those who own stock; stakeholders can include employees, volunteers, lenders, and so on.

Stock option   A right afforded by a corporation for an organization or individual to purchase a set amount of shares at a specified price over a fixed period of time.

Traditional model   A model of governance in which the board of directors appoints an executive to run the organization. Another key feature of this model is that the board governs the executive through the establishment of subcommittees of directors. This model is similar to the Carver model, although that model of governance does not include the establishment of committees.

Trust   A legal document established to ensure that a charitable act is carried out as part of an estate.

Securities and Exchange Commission (SEC)   A U.S. government organization created by the Securities Exchange Act of 1934.

White knight   A company that enters a bidding war for a corporation's shares during the threat of a hostile takeover. The white knight either gains control of the corporation or drives the price of the shares up to a more reasonable sale value for the shareholders.

XBRL   Formerly known as extensible business reporting language, this is an XML-based standard for defining and exchanging financial information.

Index

Index

F

Failures, Board, 96, 104
Foreign Board Members, 50
Foreign Issuers, 194
Foundation, 194
Fraud, 11, 23, 55, 136, 161, 164
FTSE, 185
Full Disclosure, 172

G

Generally Accepted Accounting Principles (GAAP),
194–195
Global Corporate Governance Forum, 195
Global Depositary Receipts (GDR's), 195
Governance Model, 14, 86

H

Health Insurance Portability and Accountability Act
(HIPPA), 195
Hostile Takeovers, 19–24, 116, 117, 195

I

IBM, 181
Implementation, 23, 89, 114, 129, 146
Income, Taxation on, 6
Incorporation, 6, 165
Insider Trading, 23, 53
Institute on Governance, 190
Instituto Argentino para el Gobierno de las
Organiaciones, 195
Interlocks, 195
Internal Controls, 191
International Corporate Governance Network, 196
International Financial Reporting Standards, 195

L

Labor Relations, 44, 84, 147, 148, 167
Lay, Kenneth, 111
Liability Insurance, 54
Limited Liability Corporations (LLCs), 196
Limited Liability Partnership (LLP), 196
Limited Partners, 196

M

Management Model, 196
Markets, 7, 18, 66, 82, 109, 142, 146
Mergers, 41

N

National Institute of Standards and Technology
(NIST), 196
Nike, 12
Non-Profit Organizations, 35, 163–177, 189
Novo Mercado, 197

O

Organization for Economic Co-operation and
Development, 190
Outsourcing, xx

P

Partnerships, 5, 64, 122, 146, 156, 169, 197
Payment, 6, 30
Penalties, 109, 147
Performance Evaluation, 107, 114, 186
Poison Pill, 197
Proprietorship, 198
Public Company Accounting Oversight Board
(PCAOB), 111

R

Regulation 14a-8, 197
Reprisal, 36, 39, 54–55
Restricted Stock, 197
Restructuring, 108
Revenues, 22, 192

S

Salaries, 53, 115
Santa Clara v. Southern Pacific Railroad, ix, 22
Securities Act (1933), 22
Securities and Exchange Commission, 23–24, 31, 56,
65, 104, 109, 121, 199
Securities Exchange (1934), 22
Severance Packages, 70
Shanghai Stock Exchange (SHSE)
Shareholder proposal, 199
Shareholders, responsibilities of, 5–15, 20, 29–37
Skilling, Jeffery, x
Society of Corporate Secretaries and Governance
Professionals, 190
Solutions, 55
Stakeholder, 199
Stakeholders, 9, 19, 35, 47, 90, 105, 119, 122,
165–177
Stock Option, 199
Stock Options, 46, 53, 66, 187

T

Traditional Model, 199
Trusts, 166

W

Wealth, 85, 149
White Knight, 199

X

XBRL, 199